PAPER SLOYD

FOR PRIMARY GRADES

CHILDREN IN THE PRIMARY GRADES AT WORK ON PAPER SLOYD MODELS

PAPER SLOYD

A HANDBOOK
FOR PRIMARY GRADES

by

Ednah Anne Rich

YESTERDAY'S CLASSICS

ITHACA, NEW YORK

Cover and arrangement © 2017 Yesterday's Classics, LLC.

This edition, first published in 2017 by Yesterday's Classics, an imprint of Yesterday's Classics, LLC, is an unabridged republication of the text originally published by Ginn and Company in 1905. For the complete listing of the books that are published by Yesterday's Classics, please visit www.yesterdaysclassics.com. Yesterday's Classics is the publishing arm of the Baldwin Online Children's Literature Project which presents the complete text of hundreds of classic books for children at www.mainlesson.com.

ISBN: 978-1-63334-093-0

Yesterday's Classics, LLC
PO Box 339
Ithaca, NY 14851

PREFACE

This little book is written with the thought that it may help teachers and parents who desire to teach children such constructive work in paper as is comprehensible in the first primary grades. Its publication is designed to give right training and happiness to many little children, thereby extending the good work of Miss Anna S. C. Blake, to whose generosity the author is indebted for much valuable experience as sloyd teacher and supervisor of manual training.

Miss Anna S. C. Blake established in Santa Barbara, California, in 1891-1892, the first manual training on the Pacific coast for public-school classes (sewing and cooking for girls, wood sloyd for boys), and maintained the same until her death in 1899, — the work having been previously adopted into the regular curriculum of the city schools.

Miss Blake's idea that there should be no break in the hand and eye training from the kindergarten to the fourth grade, where wood sloyd and sewing properly begin, encouraged the working out of the series of simple models herein pictured and described. Seven years of experience with classes, varying in size from ten to forty, girls and boys, taught in the class room by grade teachers, have brought satisfactory results.

The name "paper sloyd" was first applied to this course of constructive work by the primary teachers and pupils who recognized the training as a preparation for the wood sloyd and the sewing. Experience in teaching paper sloyd brought a broader conception of the value of the work in its relation to other subjects and in itself, and the name has been retained because it clearly expresses the significance of the training to be given through this suggestive series of models.

The Century Dictionary, describing the origin of the word "sloyd" or "sloid" and its application to a special system of wood-work, adds: "It is not confined to wood-working, as is frequently supposed (though this is the branch most commonly taught), but is work with the hands and with simple tools."

Paper sloyd is only one form of manual training, but it means more than the mere mechanical construction of models; therefore the definition of sloyd given by the Sloyd Training School, Boston, has been adopted, with the omission of the word "vigorous," which is included when we substitute "wood" for "paper": " Sloyd is tool work so arranged and employed as to stimulate and promote vigorous, intelligent self-activity *for a purpose*, which the worker recognizes as good."

The models are interesting, useful, plain, and simple in construction. Some of them were suggested by articles of wood and others by familiar forms, but in every case the proportion and measurements are the product of careful study on the author's part, as is the whole plan of work which, unpublished, has been in everyday use in city and country schools for six or more years.

Grateful acknowledgment is here made to those primary teachers who, during the experimental stages of the work, aided in the practical demonstration of the problems which confront the introduction of any course of study, and who have by their interest and coöperation helped to make the paper sloyd a real part of each child's development along right lines.

The simplicity of equipment and the use of inexpensive material in the construction of paper-sloyd models eliminate the question of expense, — one of the greatest obstacles to the introduction of manual training into the crowded first primary classes. This handbook comes with suggestions to those familiar with constructive work, and through its explicit directions makes possible the teaching of this series of models by any earnest instructor who is ready to put forth an effort to "learn by doing."

The book aims to give practical assistance to those who are seeking advancement for their pupils, but it carries also an earnest plea for thoughtful individual effort on the part of the teacher in behalf of each child who is "going forward and upward step by step."

EDNAH ANNE RICH

The Anna S. C. Blake Manual Training School

Santa Barbara, California

June, 1905

INTRODUCTION

In most school systems of importance throughout the country to-day promising experiments in manual training are under way, and in them all manual training is rapidly winning a respectable place. As our experiments proceed we are learning that this form of training has not only a specific educational value, that it develops not only manual dexterity, an important and obvious result, but that it has also a valuable tonic effect on the pupil throughout the whole process of his general education, — on the development of his powers of observation, assimilation, and expression.

This general as well as specific educational value of manual training has long been claimed for it by its advocates; but the experimental demonstration of the validity of this claim, even with our far from satisfactory contemporary schemes of manual training, is daily becoming more convincing.

We are coming to see that the pursuit and attainment by the pupil of a concrete end — some object constructed by him in accordance with a clearly conceived plan — involves a general training as useful in itself and as serviceable in its permanent effect on the pupil as the attainment of a purely intellectual end, — the successful pursuit of a language, the effective grappling with some social problem, or with a problem in natural science or in mathematics, each in its own sphere. This is the meaning of the widespread recognition of manual training in our contemporary programmes of study and the rapidly growing expenditures for the adequate and appropriate instruction of this "subject," particularly in the upper grammar and high school grades. In those grades, also, the important value of manual training as a means of discovering and developing special aptitude for constructive work, of teaching the pupil the importance of hand work as well as head work, and the supreme importance of the combination of the two, are winning increasing and appropriate recognition.

Moreover, in every grade, its stimulative effect (formerly commonly unsuspected) in awakening peculiar or sluggish minds and its wholesome curative influence on abnormal or defective pupils are not less apparent than the specific and general influences on all minds, referred to above.

In short, we are coming to see that manual training is an exceedingly valuable educational instrument in dealing with minds of all types and in every stage of development. To use this instrument of education most effectively, we still need a well-planned scheme of "construction work" covering every grade from the kindergarten through the high school. Two conspicuous difficulties are met by all who have such a scheme to plan, namely, (1) to make such a choice of materials and processes as will satisfy the child's natural demand for progressive continuity in the interest and difficulty of the work he has to do; and (2) at the same time to enable him to appreciate with increasing adequacy the social significance of constructive activities in modern life.

Meanwhile very few of the originators of schemes proposed or now in operation are satisfied with them. These schemes are acknowledged to be provisional or temporary only, serving, however, the useful purpose of intelligent experimentation. In particular it has been found very difficult to devise a series of exercises with appropriate materials for the earliest school years. The materials to be employed, the nature of the exercises themselves, and the best way to articulate the work throughout with the kindergarten work on the one hand and the grammar-school work on the other, and, above all, how to make the work contribute in a simple yet serious way to the final realization of the full educational value of manual training, are problems whose complete solution is yet to be sought. Nevertheless, every thoughtful worker brings us a little nearer the end we are seeking. The amount of thought and individual experimenting now devoted to every phase of manual training is full of promise, and I welcome Miss Rich's book as a valuable contribution to the solution of the problem with which it deals.

This book seems to offer to teachers, by the special field which it covers, by the variety and practicability of the exercises which it provides, and by the suggestions it contains for the extension and improvement of manual training for primary-school children, a good manual of instruction and an excellent basis for the intelligent experimentation which it is desirable everywhere to promote.

PAUL H. HANUS

LIST OF PAPER SLOYD MODELS
FOR PRIMARY GRADES

FIRST-YEAR MODELS

SECOND-YEAR MODELS

THIRD-YEAR MODELS

THIRD-YEAR MODELS

SUPPLEMENTARY MODELS

PAPER SLOYD FOR PRIMARY GRADES

This manual is designed for use in the *first three* grades of public or private schools in city, town, or country. Older children studying at home may use the book with profit, while parents will find the construction work interesting and beneficial training for the younger children.

Paper sloyd, regarded as a subject in itself, not as "busy work," should have a place in the course of study with clay modeling, free-hand drawing, and brush work.

The value of this branch of manual training is greater than one who knows nothing of hand work might believe; but the importance of its place in the curriculum is relative, depending in a measure on the needs of the pupils in the special district or locality in which the paper sloyd is being taught. All children, foreigners as well, enjoy the hand work intensely, because in it they find expression and can see the result of their efforts.

The book presupposes little or no knowledge of construction work and no experience in teaching the same; hence the information as to materials, equipment, etc., the explanation of the several operations in construction, suggestions as to methods of presentation, and the careful working directions or dictations are most explicit.

The manual training teacher may find suggestive models, and the supervisor can put the book into the hands of his grade teachers, who must give instruction to their large classes, knowing that the principles are right.

The series of models is carefully arranged with regard to form, proportion, measurements, and construction, and is designed as a preparation for the wood sloyd, or bench work in wood, for boys and the sewing for girls, which *should begin in the fourth grade.*

Through this construction work the teacher should establish a close relation with language and with number. Simple combinations and fractions, learned with the paper sloyd models for the object, are easily mastered and readily applied in the formal number work later.

Prompt obedience to requests for attention and immediate response to dictation, be the lesson in whatever subject, are essential in the school life of to-day, and these important qualities paper sloyd helps to develop. Order, neatness about the work, carefulness, accuracy, honesty, — important factors in any school, — follow in the lead of all work which trains to concentration of attention.

Observation is quickened; eyes are trained to see right lines and distances, thus aiding in free-hand drawing and writing; while the hand and wrist muscles, being used for a definite purpose, unconsciously become obedient assistants. Paper sloyd rightly presented justifies itself.

All beginners in paper sloyd need a certain amount of drill in measuring; but that does not mean that the pupils should be kept the whole lesson period drawing lines of varying lengths nor repeating over and over the names of the several divisions. The teacher must be patient during the first part of the year and realize that manual work is brain work as well, and that the hand and eye must become used to giving quick response to the directions of the mind. The subject should be developed as carefully as language, writing, and free-hand drawing.

First-grade pupils should think of their measure as a ruler and accept the fact that it is one foot — twelve inches — long. Allow them to balance the ruler on the forefinger, and they will quickly show you the middle. Direct them to put the thumb nail or finger nail on the **6″** line, showing them the line on your own ruler, and tell them that **6″** is the middle. They do not know figures and will not realize that the figure **6** has any meaning, but they will remember the line and its name. Further proof that **6″** is half of **12″** may be demonstrated by holding the ruler vertically with the thumb nail on the **6″** mark and quickly passing the forefinger of the right hand from the top down to the **6″** and from the bottom up to the **6″**. Narrow strips of paper may be measured with the ruler, creased and torn, then folded in the middle. Allow the pupil to *feel* the length of the space on the ruler by passing his finger several times

down the edge; then, quickly putting the ruler into his desk, let him *see* the space by placing the forefinger of each hand six inches apart on the front edge of the desk. The teacher, passing quickly from desk to desk, measures these spaces and allows the pupil to make any necessary correction by moving the right-hand finger. Lines **12″** and **6″** may be drawn with chalk on the blackboard, lines the same lengths laid with sticks on the desk, etc. There are many ways to develop the measure to be used, and these suggestions are merely given because they have been found useful. The ruler drill, or play, can be made a helpful part of school work and may occupy four or five moments of any period.

Though there should be no *preliminary* lessons as *abstract exercises*, the steps in making the first model should go *very slowly*; and it may be well to make several models from ordinary manila scratch paper before using the manila drawing paper, which is a little harder to fold and to crease.

The lesson periods—*twenty, thirty,* and *forty* minutes—*seem* short, and both teacher and pupil are loath to put away the work at the close, since it is not easy to wait a week before seeing the finished model nor agreeable for the teacher to interrupt when the interest is so keenly aroused. There is a lesson in promptness, and in not allowing one subject to crowd upon another, but more important is the consideration of the question of fatigue which manifests itself in restlessness on the children's part and unconscious impatience in the teacher. The interest will be all the more intense if held in abeyance from week to week, lesson to lesson.

The repetition of the square in the first-year models is not monotonous, since the interest is held not by the form, but by the name of the model and its significance. The short lines make folding and cutting easy, and without any special drill the pupils find each of the **1″** marks, so by the time they are ready to use the same, they know that there are twelve spaces on a foot ruler. The half inch is taught as half of the inch space and may be remembered at first by the difference in the length of the division lines of ½″ and **1″**. The quarter, or fourth, inch is developed from the half, and the eighth inch from the fourth objectively, by the use of the ruler. Children slow to see divisions are ofttimes helped by likening the inch and its parts to the dollar, half dollar, and quarter.

Curved outlines are omitted until the third year, because the pupil has not sufficient muscular control to use the compass readily; his training in measuring would be more hampered if the outlines were broken; and at this period his free-hand drawing is giving him the best of training in the matter of curves and circles.

Innumerable articles may be made of paper, and those included in this series should suggest others. Pasteboard doll houses with furniture give great pleasure to their owners and occupy many happy hours at home. Such a line of work is acceptable in the schoolroom if it is correlated with other subjects and promotes the spirit of coöperation.

Gifts for special occasions may be made at school. Familiar forms constructed of different paper sometimes satisfy the worker.

Encourage the making of "inventions" or "original models" and in countless ways help the children to feel that this hand work has a real part in their school life and in their homes.

Type forms as abstract lessons are left out of this series of models, as are the fancy, scalloped, ribbon-tied trays, boxes, and baskets which seemingly have no place in the *first* primary grades, — the years in which constructive work in paper *should be taught* to *every* boy and girl.

The fact that there are few toys and articles for the child's own use among the models has, after six years' trial, proven no mistake. Children gain truest happiness in making those things which give pleasure to the people in the home and establish for them the appreciated position of contributors to the household.

EQUIPMENT AND MATERIAL

Equipment. — Pencil, ruler, scissors, pencil compass, punch.

Material. — Manila drawing or drafting paper, 60 lbs.; Bristol board, 3 ply; Royal Melton or other cover paper, sandpaper (No. 1), blotting paper; yarn, cord, twine, ribbon, for ties; library, art, or photo paste in bottles or tubes; gummed parquetry circles and squares, and gummed stars.

EQUIPMENT

Pencils. — The pencils, medium, with erasers in the ends, should be kept sharpened and used solely for paper sloyd drawings. Pieces of pasteboard, with elastic sewed on in as many loops as there are desks in a row, make convenient holders and facilitate distribution.

Ruler. — Ruler twelve inches long, hard wood, light weight, back edge square, front edge beveled, divisions not less than eighths. A primary ruler, marked with **1″**, **½″**, **¼″**, is satisfactory for the first two years.

Scissors. — Scissors, nickel plated, five inches long, one point sharp, one blunt, should be kept in cases. Allow one pair of scissors to each child or one for every two children. A scissors case, twelve inches wide, may be made of single width gray Canton flannel. Hem the edges, fold lengthwise (lap piece, four and one-half inches wide), and stitch pockets for scissors and one for punch and chamois. The cloth at the top folds over when the scissors are in place, and the whole may be made into a compact roll. Scissors should be wiped with chamois after using.

Pencil Compass. — A compass attachment slipped onto the pencil when necessary to draw curves or circles. Supply compass point for each child.

Punch. — Nickel-plated conductor's punch making a round hole three sixteenths of an inch or less in diameter. Only one punch is necessary with each equipment.

MATERIAL

Manila drawing or drafting paper, rated at sixty pounds, may be purchased by the ream. Choose paper with rough surface, tough and strong, that can be folded and creased easily by small children. Laid Antique Cover is also satisfactory paper.

Bristol board, three ply, is easily cut with scissors, folds with light scoring, and does not break when creased. There is a wide choice in colors. The geranium (red), lavender, blue-gray, and gray are satisfactory. It is purchased by the hundred sheets; sheets, 22 × 28 inches.

Royal Melton, seventy pounds, or other cover papers in colors — olive green, gray, brown, and red — are purchased by the sheet, 20 × 25 inches.

Sandpaper (Number 1), for match scratchers, 8 × 12 inches.

Blotting paper, color buff, may be bought by the sheet.

This list enumerates some of the inexpensive material for construction work, and is intended to be suggestive merely. Paper of many grades and textures may be procured in beautiful and delicate shades and tints.

Gummed Parquetry. — Circles and squares (color dark red), one inch in diameter, bought in packages (one hundred in a package) from kindergarten supply department at any stationers.

Gummed Stars. — Small gold or colored stars may be purchased in any quantity.

Pictures. — The picture frames are designed for small photographs or the small pictures known as "half-penny pictures," which are easily procured and may be chosen with reference to the year's picture study.

Ties. — Yarn, silk or linen floss, silk or cotton cord, ribbon, and colored twine are all available, preference being given to the first and last because of their suitableness for use with the inexpensive paper.

Paste. — Library, art, or photograph paste is satisfactory and, when purchased in large quantities, inexpensive. Small tubes or bottles may be provided for each pupil, or he may be served from a large bottle, sufficient paste being placed on a scrap of paper on his desk. The paste may be spread with a small brush, toothpick, or piece of stiff paper.

Preparation of Material. — All paper should be machine cut, one quarter or one half inch larger than the finished dimensions. This insures square corners and makes constructive work possible with the children in the first primary grades.

Should these designs be used in higher grades — third, fourth, and fifth — with heavier boards, the children may square the corners by use of a straight edge and triangle. These implements could, of course, be used in the lower grades, but it is not considered wise to exact so much attention to detail from young pupils. The paper will be cut at any printing office at small cost.

GENERAL DIRECTIONS

Working Plans. — Set apart a certain time — *twenty* minutes in the *first* grade, *thirty* minutes in the *second*, and *forty* minutes in the *third* — on a *certain* day *each* week for the paper sloyd lesson. Choose the period immediately following the opening hour in the morning. The children respond quickly to directions at this time. Have everything in readiness that no time will be wasted in distribution.

Suggestions. — Place on the front desk of each row the card of pencils, rulers (held in a bundle by elastic band), compasses, and as many pieces of paper as there are pupils in the row. Direct that each in turn shall be passed backward down the row, and from the back seat forward at the close of the lesson, thus avoiding noise and delay. Scissors may be passed by monitors. The injunction "Do not handle" must be enforced when tools are not in use. Require prompt attention. Give in the first months only one direction, as brief as possible, at a time, accompanying the words by an illustration — showing the required line on a drawing, either on the blackboard or on paper.

Experience shows that, in conveying to young children a definite conception of what is to be done, a simple expression oft repeated eliminates confusion of thought and brings certain muscular actions readily under control. Thus: "Place a ruler," etc., "Place a dot," etc., gains response more readily than "Measure from the left-hand side at the top of the paper and make a dot," etc.; "Draw line through the dots" brings better results from beginners than "Connect the points."

A set of models made by the teacher should be in evidence. Three or four extra models should be made by as many children each lesson, the same to be kept at the school for exhibition, each pupil being allowed to carry his model home when finished.

Position of Paper. — Unless specially mentioned, the directions for all of the models presuppose that the paper is placed on the desk with the *long* edge horizontal or parallel to the front edge of the desk. The edges of the paper are then designated as top, bottom, left, right. The position of the paper *should not be changed* until the drawing is completed. Adherence to this rule will save time, careless mistakes by the pupils, and annoyance on the part of the teacher.

Measurements read from the left and top edges of the paper, except on the inside lines, when the end of the ruler is placed on the dot, as noted in directions.

The directions for making the envelope are to be followed in the construction of all succeeding plain models except where otherwise specified. "Construct a square" means that the directions for placing the ruler, placing dots, and drawing lines, given under the first drawing, are to be repeated.

WORKING DIRECTIONS

Ruler. — The ruler must at all times be held firmly. Teach the children to place the thumb and first two or three fingers of the left hand on the ruler, stretching them wide apart, and holding the hand nearly at right angles to the arm, which does not touch the desk. Small children whose desk tops are too high should be allowed to stand.

Position of Pencil. — Direct the pupil when drawing lines with the ruler to draw against the beveled edge, — to hold his pencil firmly and draw the line lightly and quickly, as if with one stroke. Overcome the tendency of little children to make large dots by directing them to hold the pencil as straight as possible and turn it a little one way, then the other, pressing lightly. Direct lines to be drawn through the dots, using any comparison that will impress the pupils with the clearness and trueness of the line, — a railroad track, a fence, etc.

Pencil Compass. — Adjust the metal point onto the pencil, the points of each being even, and open to the required dimensions; place the point on the dot; keep the paper in position with the left hand; hold the pencil near the end with the right hand and draw the curve quickly and lightly.

Folding. — Place the ruler on the line, the pencil mark showing above the edge; hold firmly as directed. With the right hand lift the side of the paper to be folded; slip the thumb under; bring the same to a vertical position; pass the thumb nail along the paper, pressing it square against the ruler; remove the ruler; fold the paper flat and crease sharply with the finger nail of the second finger held flat on the desk and kept in position by the thumb; release and the side will form a right angle. The importance of folding and creasing cannot be overestimated. Often a good model is spoiled in the finishing because the fold is soiled or not sharp, owing to the ends of the fingers being used instead of the finger nail. Score (draw the line lightly with the blunt point of scissors) before folding stiff or heavy paper.

Cutting. — Place the paper in first position; take it in the left hand; hold it firmly at the bottom with the thumb in front and the fingers at the back; cut the line at the right from bottom to top; change the position of the left hand if the line is long or the paper not stiff; turn the paper until all the outlines are cut, then put it again in the first position; cut from the bottom to the inside lines, turning the paper as each side is finished. Never turn the scissors at a corner; cut to the point from both sides; cut half circles from the middle downward on each side. Pupils who need practice may be encouraged to cut, at home, lines on newspapers.

Punching. — A teacher having large classes, with limited time for the lessons, may punch the holes in the models. The holes should be near the edge and as even as possible.

Names.—The pupil's name should be written or printed in small letters inside, on the bottom, or in some inconspicuous place. Space of one eighth inch or three sixteenths is allowed for printing.

A simple letter is made by combination of straight lines and curves : thus B should be printed F, then B; D, I, then D; S, ≡, then S. Call the children's attention to the similarity in construction of the letters B, E, F, P, R; of J, U, and G, C, O. Require the letters to fill the space between the lines. The printing of names should not begin until the third year, primarily because all the writing movements should be large and free the first years; the vertical writing and the printing may be confused one with the other, and the pupils do not know the smaller divisions of the ruler.

Tying.—Give each child a tie of sufficient length to knot into all the corners; allow him to cut it into the required number of pieces. A flat knot with short ends is quite as satisfactory as a bow knot. Loops for hanging should not be too long. The simpler the tie the better, for then there is a suggestion to the child that everyday material at home has a value.

Pasting. — First fold the model, with few exceptions laps inside; find the sides to be pasted; spread the paste over the whole surface of the lap, paying special attention to edges and corners; fit carefully; smooth with the finger nails; pass the ruler over the surface if desired; trim uneven edges. Pasted models which are flat should be placed under a book for a short time, and boxes fitted closely together into a large pasteboard box to keep the sides from warping.

I. ENVELOPE. 6″ × 6″

Place the ruler on the paper just below the top, even at the left; place a dot at **6″**. Slip the ruler to the bottom of the paper, even at the left; place a dot at **6″**. Draw a light line through the dots from top to bottom.

Place the ruler on the left side of the paper, even at the top; place a dot at **6″**. Place the ruler on the right, even at the top; place a dot at **6″**. Draw a light line through the dots from left to right.

Holding the paper at the bottom, cut the line at the right from bottom to top; turn paper to the right, and cut on the line.

Place the paper on the desk in the first position; place the ruler across the paper touching the upper left and lower right corners; draw a light line. Place ruler on lower left and upper right corners; draw a line. Fold upper left corner to the center; fold opposite corner; fold the other corners.

Inclose a letter in the envelope and seal the corners with **1″** circle of gummed parquetry. Write address on the front and, if desired, paste a canceled stamp in the upper right corner.

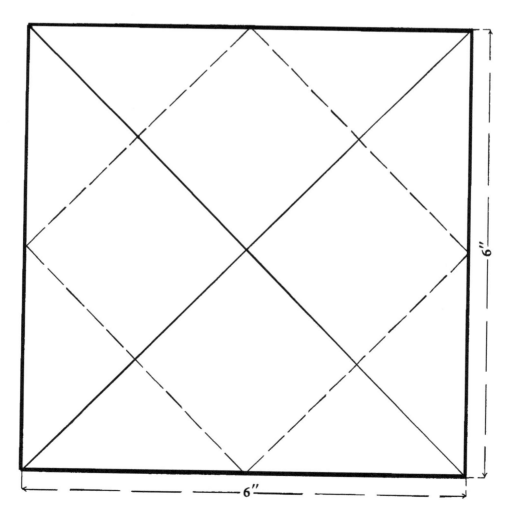

II. WALL POCKET. 6″ × 6″

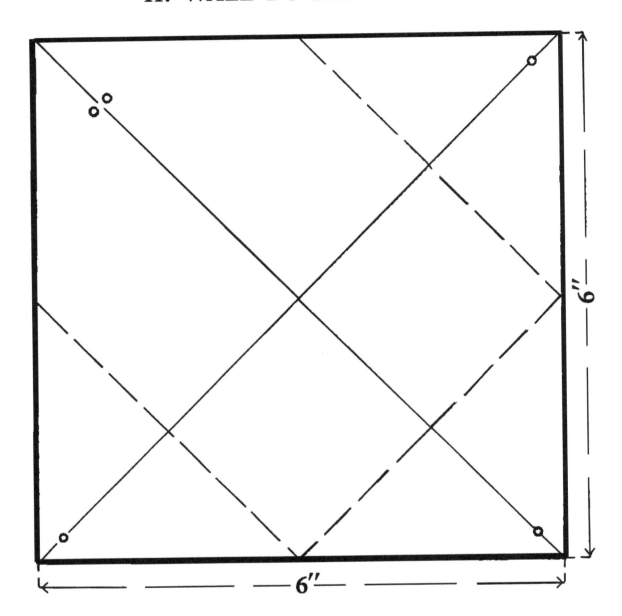

Construct a square **6″** × **6″**.

Draw lines from corner to corner.

Fold three corners to the center.

Punch holes on the lines near the corners for the cord.

Place a dot on the line **1″** from the upper left corner.

Punch holes close together on each side of the dot.

Tie a cord through the holes to form a loop for the hanger.

Tie the corners together for the pocket.

III. PICTURE FRAME. 6″ × 6″

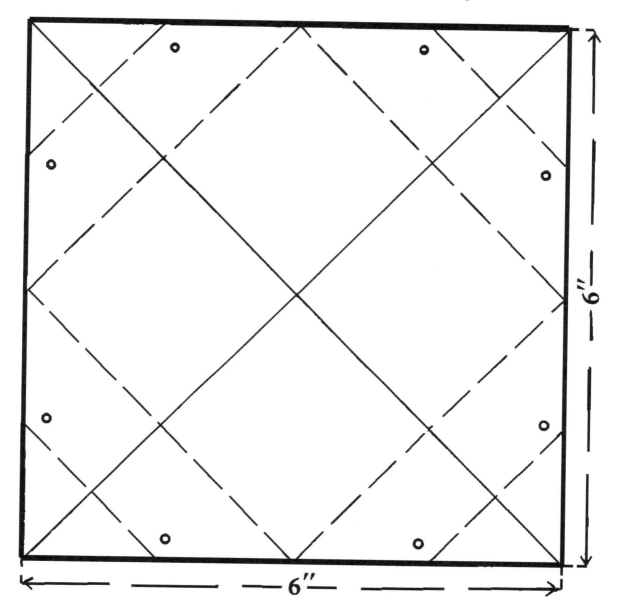

Construct a square **6″ × 6″**.

Draw lines from corner to corner.

Fold the corners to the center; open the paper and fold the points to the middle of the creased line; turn the points back and crease the fold; close the sides again.

Punch holes for the ties.

Tie with cord, ribbon, floss, or yarn in flat knots or bowknots.

Children may bring pictures, or the teacher may furnish half-penny pictures.

IV. PINWHEEL. 6″ × 6″

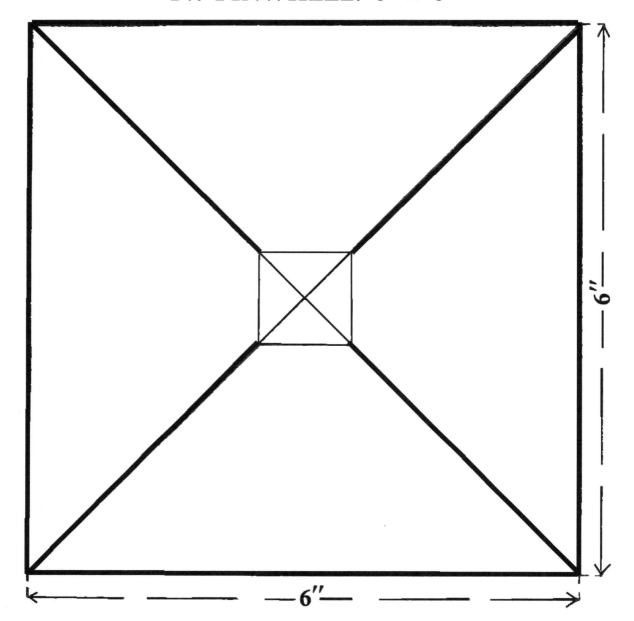

Construct a square **6″ × 6″**.

Draw lines from corner to corner.

Prick a hole in the center with a pin.

Fit a **1″** square of gummed parquetry over the center—the corners touching the diagonals.

Cut on the slanting lines to the parquetry.

Stick a pin through corners and center into the stick, which each child should bring to the class.

A twig from a tree is a satisfactory standard.

V. SCISSORS CASE. **6″ × 6″**

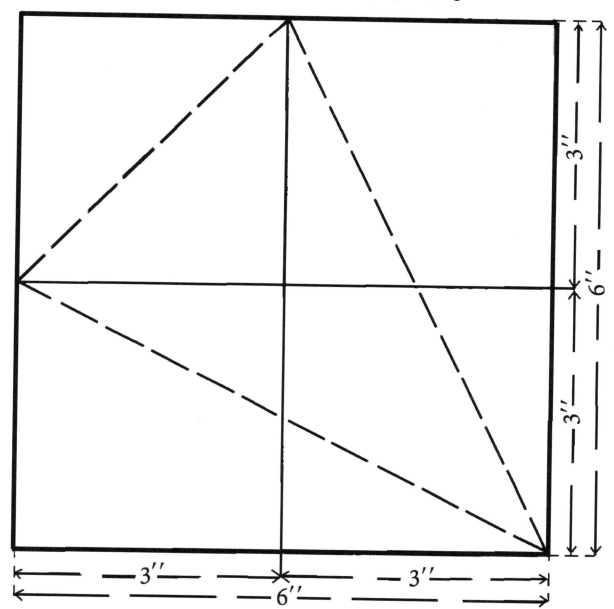

Construct a square **6″ × 6″**.

Place a dot on the top and bottom at **3″**; draw a line.

Place dots on the left and right at **3″**; draw a line connecting dots. Fold the lower left corner from the middle of the left side to the lower right corner.

Fold the upper right corner from the middle of the top to the lower right corner.

Paste together, leaving room for scissors.

Fold the upper corner over.

VI. TRAY. 6″ × 6″

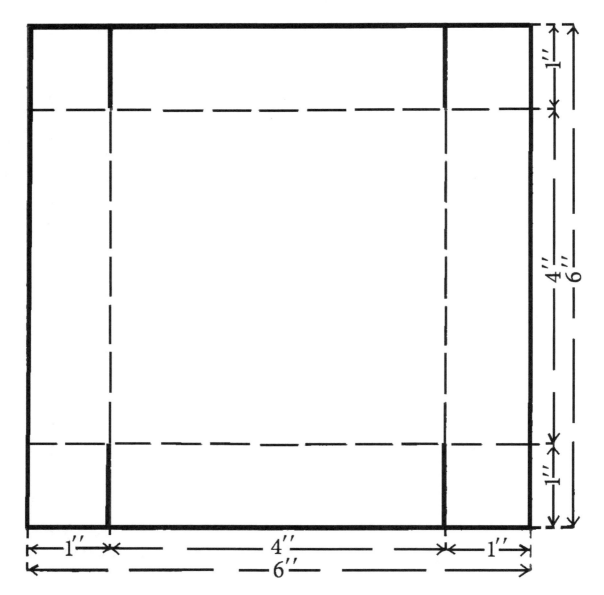

Construct a square **6″ × 6″**.

Place dots on the top and bottom at **1″**, **5″**; draw lines.

Place dots on the left and right at **1″**, **5″**; draw lines.

Cut vertical lines, top and bottom, from the outside to the inner square.

Hold the ruler on the lines, fold and crease.

Paste the laps inside, fitting each corner carefully.

VII. BOOKMARK OR BOOK CORNER. 2″ × 4″

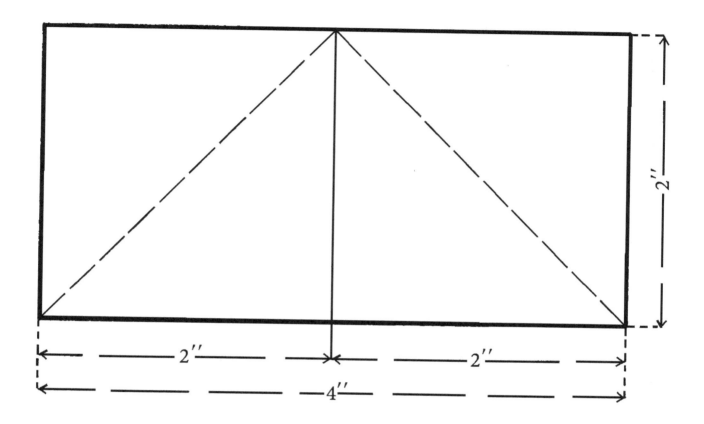

Construct an oblong **2″ × 4″**.

Place dots on the top and bottom at **2″**; draw a line.

Fold the upper left corner to the middle of the bottom.

Fold the upper right corner to the same point.

Fasten the edges together with three gummed stars or two gummed parquetry triangles.

Holes may be punched and the edges tied together with yarn.

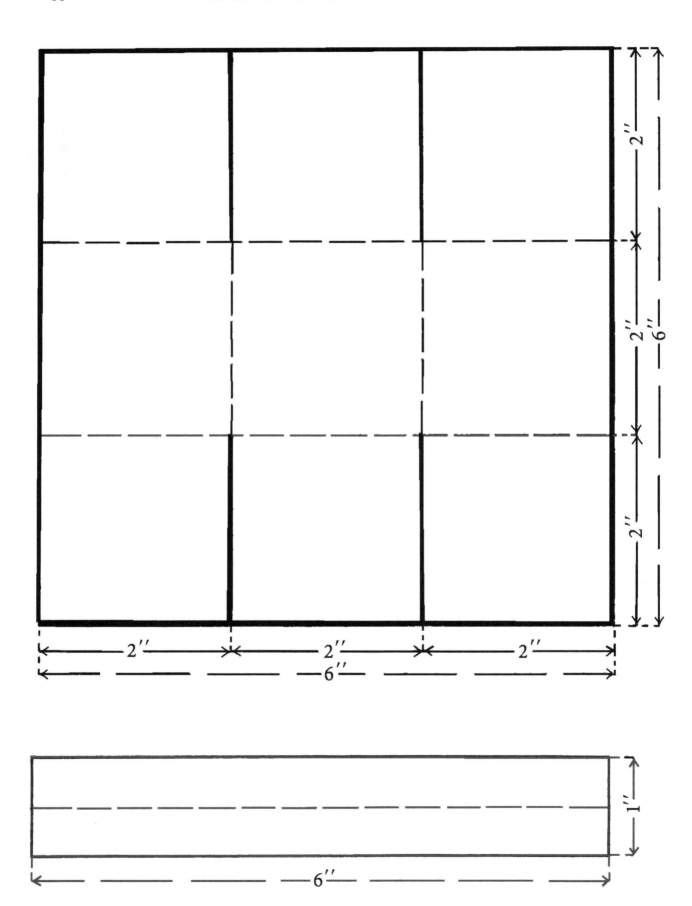

VIII. BASKET. 6″ × 6″

Construct a square **6″ × 6″**.

Place dots on the top and bottom at **2″, 4″**; draw lines.

Place dots on the left and right at **2″, 4″**; draw lines.

Holding the paper at the bottom, cut the lines to the center square.

Turn the paper from top to bottom and cut the lines.

Fold the sides against the ruler.

Remove the ruler and crease the folds sharply with the back of the finger nail.

Place the paper on the desk with the cut lines at the bottom and top.

Spread the paste evenly on the upper and lower right squares and fit outside the left squares.

Paste the handle onto these sides, in the middle. Spread the paste on the middle squares and fit them onto the sides over the ends of the handle.

The ruler may be used to smooth the pasted sides.

HANDLE. 1″ × 6″

Construct an oblong **1″ × 6″**.

Fold lengthwise and paste together.

Allow the paste to dry; then draw the handle over the finger to give it a good curve.

Paste the handle on the left and right sides of the basket.

IX. PENCIL BOX. 4″ × 9″

Construct an oblong **4″ × 9″**.

Place dots on the top and bottom at **1″**, **8″**; draw lines.

Place dots on the left and right at **1″**, **3″**; draw lines.

Cut the horizontal lines from the outside to the inner corners.

Fold on the lines and crease the folds.

Paste the corners, laps inside.

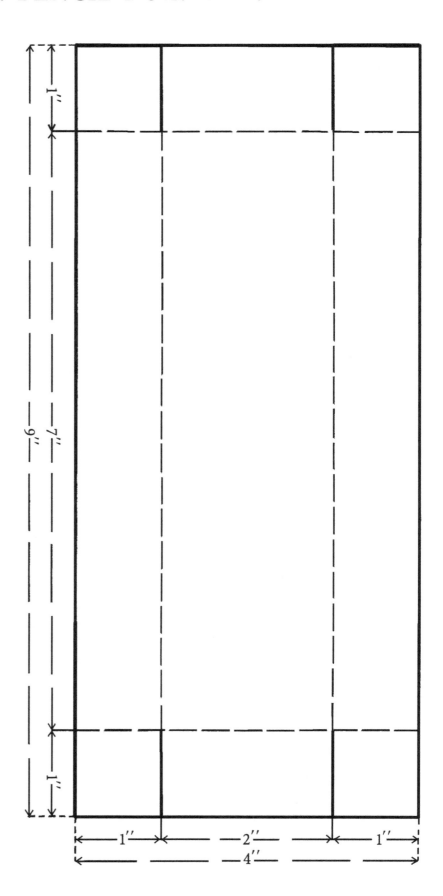

X. FAN. 6″ × 12″

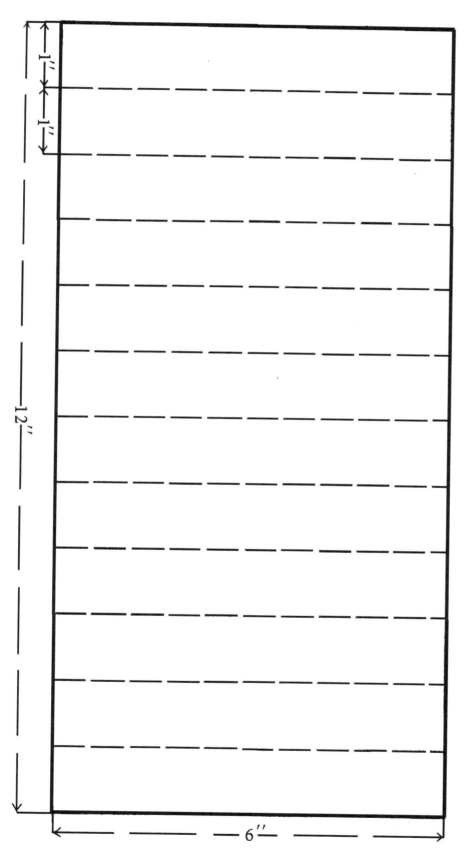

Construct an oblong **6″ × 12″** of manila paper — strong and not too heavy.

Place dots on the top and bottom at **1″, 3″, 5″, 7″, 9″, 11″**; draw lines.

Turn the paper over from top to bottom, the left and right edges being unchanged.

Place dots on the top and bottom at **2″, 4″, 6″, 8″, 10″**; draw lines.

Fold and crease the lines first on one side, then on the other.

Construct another fan in the same manner and paste together the outer folds of the two fans.

Hold the folds together and punch two holes near the bottom. Tie with a cord.

The fan may be decorated before being folded.

XI. BONBON BOX. 8″ × 8″

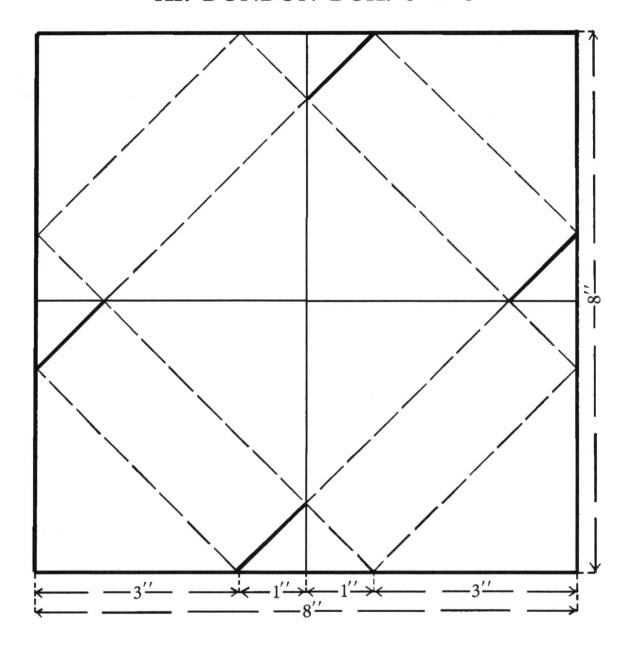

Construct a square **8″ × 8″**.

Place dots on the top and bottom at **3″, 4″, 5″**; draw lines through the middle dots.

Place dots on the left and right at **3″, 4″, 5″**; draw lines through the middle dots.

Draw slanting lines from dot to dot. (See drawing.) Cut out the corners and punch holes if the edges are to be tied, otherwise cut only the lines indicated on the drawing.

Fold on the lines and paste the laps inside.

The folded corners meeting at the center will form the cover of the box.

XII. BOOK COVER. 6″ × 8″

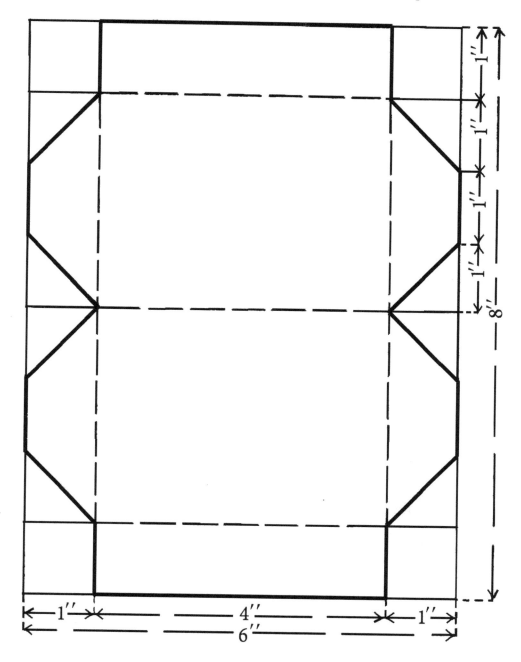

Construct an oblong **6″ × 8″**.

Place dots on the top and bottom at every inch mark; draw lines through the first, fourth, and seventh dots.

Place dots on the left and right at **1″, 5″**; draw lines.

Draw slanting lines from the corners to the dots on the edge. (See drawing.)

Cut, fold, and paste the top lap over the side lap.

XIII. BOOK SHEETS. 4″ × 6″

Cut four or more pieces of paper **4″ × 6″**; fold in the middle — each leaf being **3″ × 4″**.

Pin through the leaves from the back; fold the outer leaves back; trim off the three edges, allowing them to slip into the cover easily.

XIV. SPOOL BASKET. 6″ × 6″
(Bristol Board)

Construct a square **6″ × 6″**.

Place dots on the top and bottom at **1″, 3″, 5″**; draw lines through the first and the third dots.

Place dots on the left and right at **1″, 2″, 4″, 5″**; draw lines through the second and the third dots. Hold the ruler on the **1″** dots and on the **5″** dots and draw across the first and third spaces; draw slanting lines from the corners to the **3″** dots on the top and bottom.

Draw a short line in the middle of the sides, then cut with a knife.

Cut, fold, and paste the laps inside.

Construct a handle **½″ × 6″**.

Trim the corners; slip the ends of the handle from the outside, through the cut, into the inside of the basket, and paste.

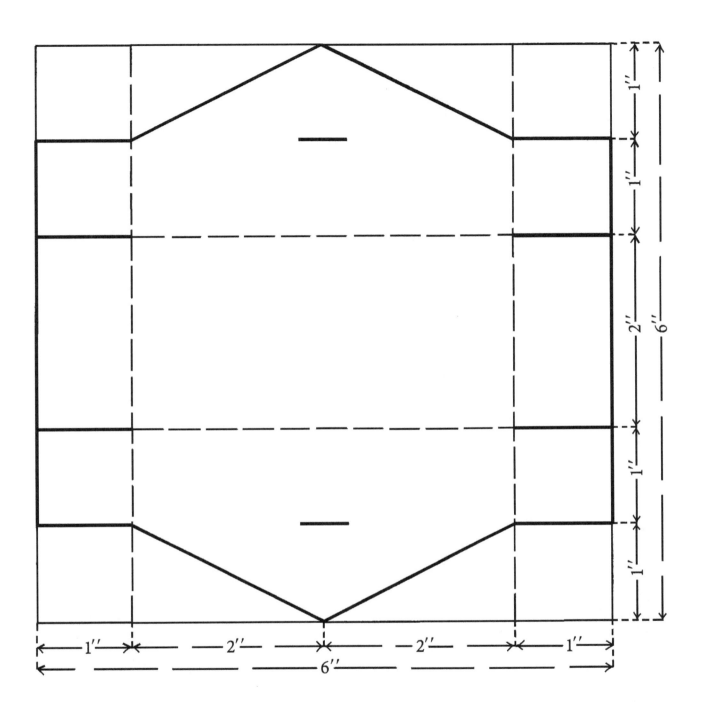

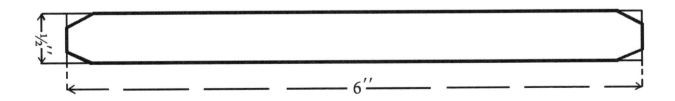

PAPER SLOYD MODELS FOR THE SECOND YEAR

I. KEY TAG. 2″ × 3½″

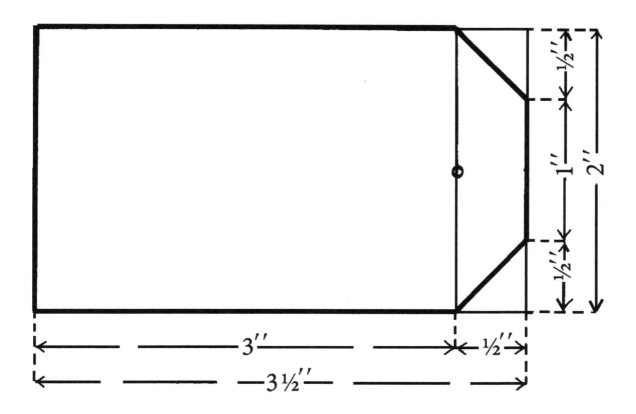

Construct an oblong **2″ × 3½″**.

Place dots on the top and bottom at **3″**.

Hold the ruler on the dots and place a dot at **1″** for a hole.

Place dots on the right edge at ½″, **1½″**; draw across the corners.

Cut the corners and punch a hole.

Cut a cord **8″** long; knot the ends together; pass the loop through the hole, and the knot through the loop.

II. STAMP BOOK. 3″ × 4½″

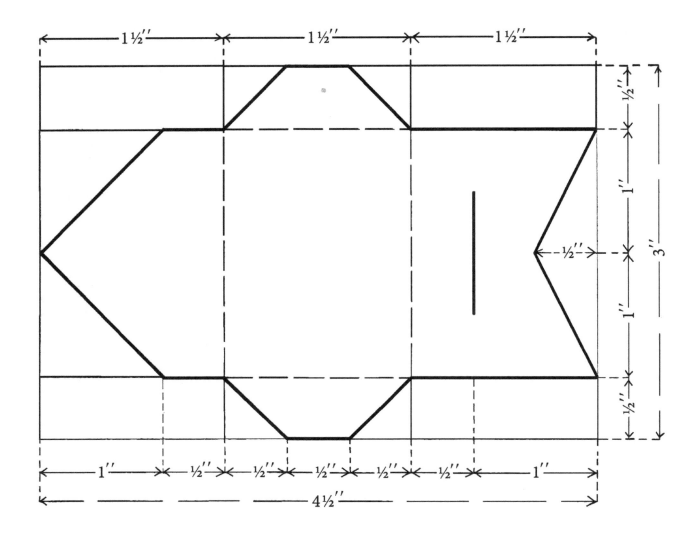

Construct an oblong **3″ × 4½″**. Place dots on the top and bottom at **1½″**, **3″**; draw lines.

Place dots on the left and right at **½″**, **2½″**; draw lines.

Place dots on the top and bottom at **2″**, **2½″**; draw to the corners.

Place dots on the left and right at **1½″**; hold the ruler on the dots and make a dot at **4″**; draw slanting lines to the right edge.

Place dots on the horizontal lines at **1″**, **3½″**; draw point at the left.

Hold the ruler on **3½″** dots and draw a line from **½″** to **1½″**.

Cut the line with a knife. Cut and fold.

Cut four pieces of paraffin paper **2″ × 3″**. Fold and pin to the fold of cover.

III. TRIANGULAR CATCH-ALL. 8″ × 8″ × 8″

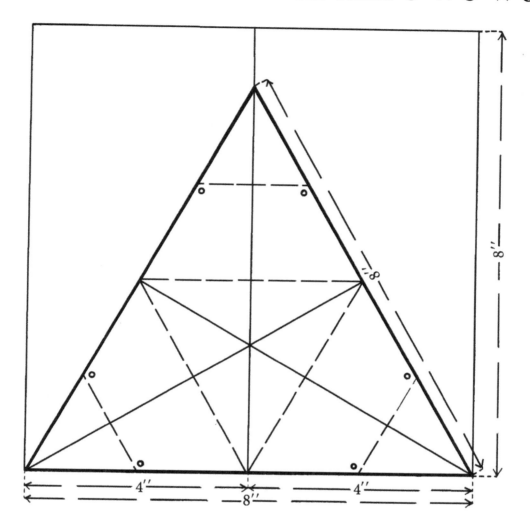

Construct a square **8″ × 8″**.

Place a dot on the top and bottom at **4″**; draw a line. Place the end of the ruler on the lower left corner, and allowing the **8″** mark to fall on the vertical line, place a dot; draw a slanting line to the dot.

Draw a line from the dot to the lower right corner. Place dots on these lines at **4″**; draw from the dots to the opposite corners.

Cut the outlines. Fold each of the corners in succession to the center point on the opposite side; crease the folds.

Open and fold the corners to the center of the creased line.

Turn the fold back and crease.

Punch holes near the edge and tie with ribbon or yarn in a flat knot or bowknot.

IV. PORTFOLIO. 9″ × 12″

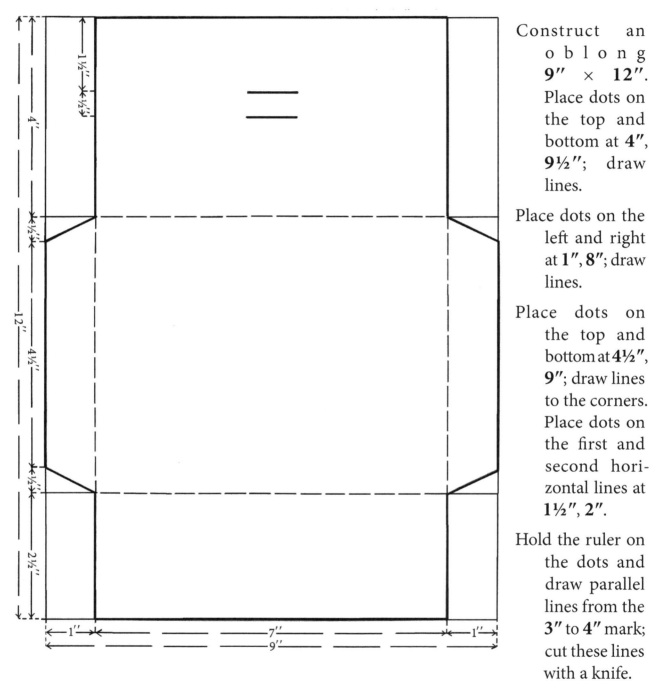

Construct an oblong **9″ × 12″**. Place dots on the top and bottom at **4″, 9½″**; draw lines.

Place dots on the left and right at **1″, 8″**; draw lines.

Place dots on the top and bottom at **4½″, 9″**; draw lines to the corners. Place dots on the first and second horizontal lines at **1½″, 2″**.

Hold the ruler on the dots and draw parallel lines from the **3″** to **4″** mark; cut these lines with a knife.

The portfolio is to be tied with a cord, one end being drawn through the slip.

V (A). THREAD WINDER. 2″ × 2″ (*Bristol Board*)

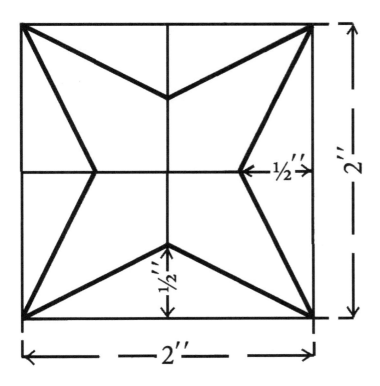

Construct a square **2″ × 2″**.

Place dots on the top, bottom, left, and right at **1″**. Connect the opposite dots.

Place dots on the horizontal and vertical lines at **½″**, **1½″**; draw from the dots to the corners.

V (B). THREAD WINDER. 2″ × 2″ (*Bristol Board*)

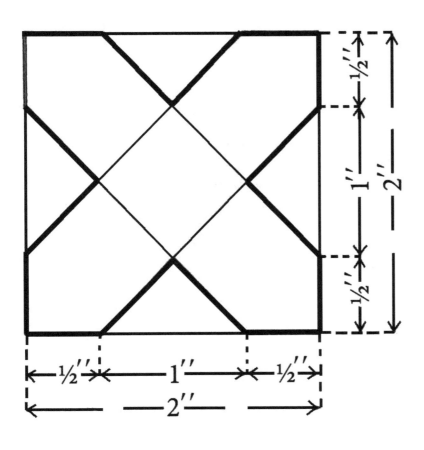

Construct a square **2″ × 2″**.

Place dots on the edge of the paper on the top, bottom, left, and right at **½″**, **1½″**.

Connect the dots. (See drawing.)

VI. MATCH SCRATCHER. 3½″ × 3½″ *(Bristol Board)*

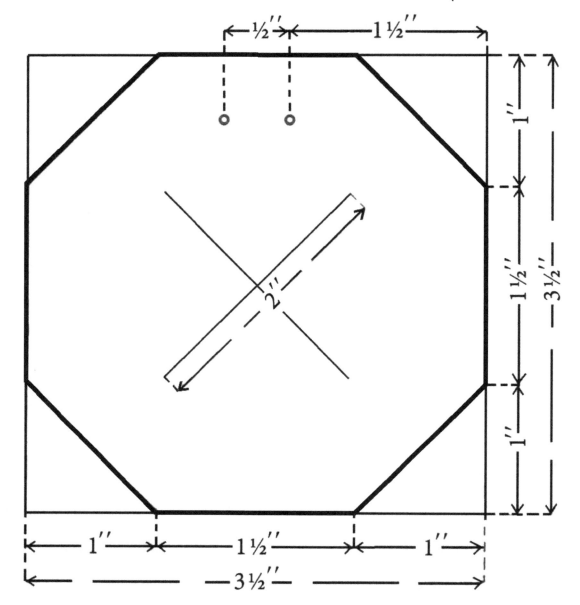

Construct a square **3½″ × 3½″**. Place dots on the edge of the paper at the top, bottom, left, and right at **1″, 2½″**; draw lines across the corners. Place a ruler across the paper on opposite corners and draw short lines to indicate the center.

Place dots on the left and right at **½″**. Hold the ruler on the dots and dot at **1½″, 2″** for holes. Cut outline. Punch holes.

Draw on the smooth side of the sandpaper a circle about **2″** in diameter. (The children may draw around some circular object.)

Cut the circle. (Special scissors should be used, since the sandpaper will dull the edge.)

Paste the sandpaper over the center.

VII. HANDKERCHIEF BOX. 5½″ × 9½″

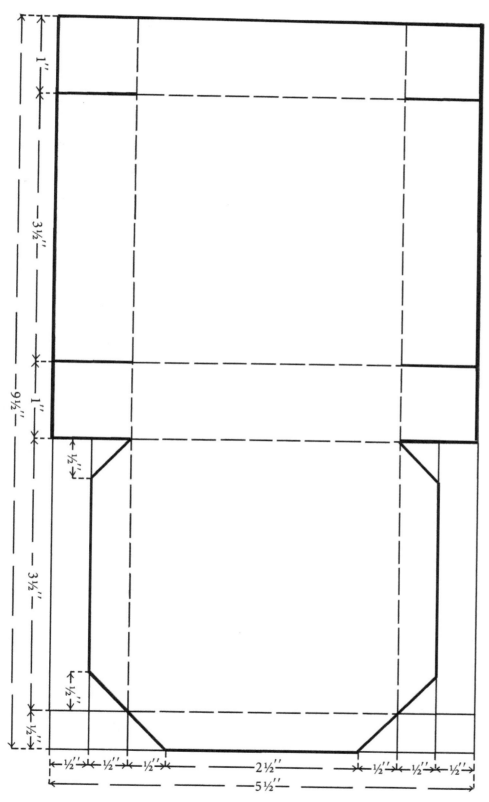

Construct an oblong **5½″ × 9½″**.

Place dots on the top and bottom at **1″, 4½″, 5½″, 9″**; draw lines.

Place dots on the left and right at **1″, 4½″**; draw lines.

Place dots on the third vertical line and the right edge at **½″, 5″**; draw lines.

Place dots on these lines at **½″, 3″**; place dots on the right edge at **1½″, 4″** and draw lines from the corners to the dots.

VIII. COMB HOLDER. 3½″ × 9″ *(Bristol Board)*

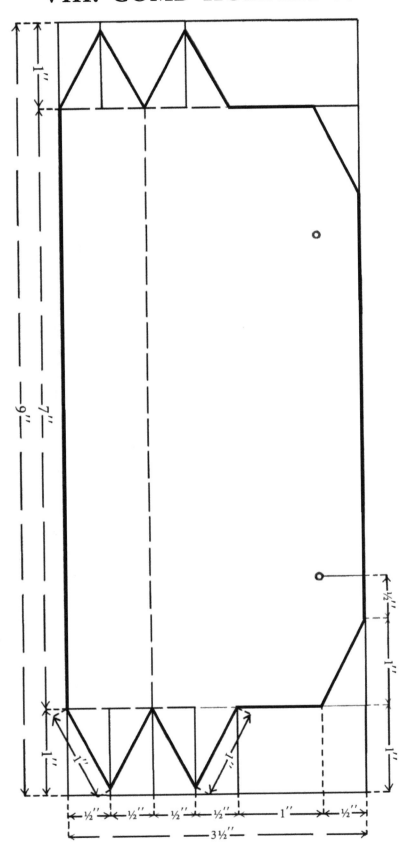

Construct an oblong **3½″ × 9″**.

Place dots on the top and bottom at **1″, 8″**; draw lines.

Place dots on the left and right at **2½″**; draw a line.

Place dots on the vertical lines at **1½″, 2″, 3″**. Hold the ruler on the dots and draw lines across the outer spaces.

Place the end of the ruler on the **1½″** dot with the **1″** mark resting on the second horizontal line; draw a slanting line; draw a line to complete the triangle.

Construct a second triangle on the left and two triangles on the right.

Place dots on the top at **2″, 7″**, and on the vertical lines at **½″**; draw lines across the corners.

Hold the ruler on the **½″** dots and place a dot at **1½″, 5½″** for the holes which are to be punched.

Cut, score the lines lightly, fold, and crease. Paste the upper triangle inside.

IX. FOLDING CARD CASE. 5″ × 11″

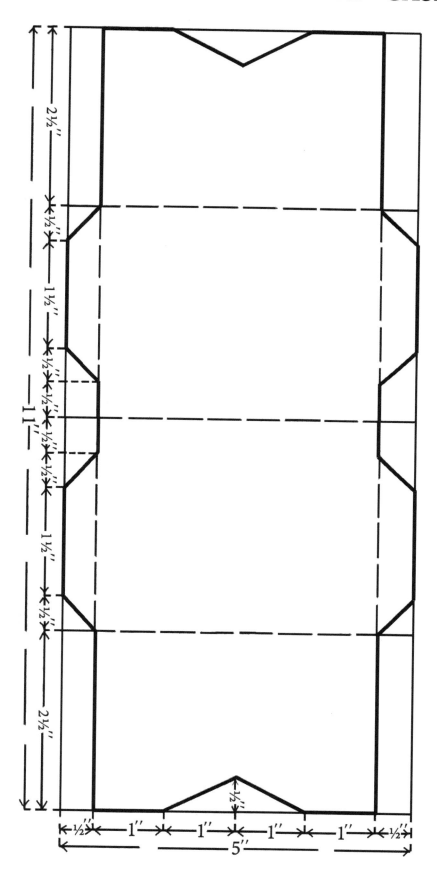

Construct an oblong **5″ × 11″**.

Place dots on the left and right at **½″, 4½″**; draw lines.

Place dots on the horizontal lines at **2½″, 5″, 5½″, 6″, 8½″**.

Connect the **2½″, 5½″, 8½″** dots.

Place dots on the top and bottom at **3″, 4½″, 6½″, 8″**; draw slanting lines to the dots on the horizontal lines. (See drawing.)

Place dots on the left and right at **1½″, 2½″, 3½″**.

Hold the ruler on the **2½″** dots and place dots at **½″, 10½″**; draw slanting lines to the dots on the edge.

Cut, fold, and paste the laps inside.

X. ENVELOPE. 7″ × 10½″

Construct an oblong **7″ × 10½″**.

Place dots on the top and bottom at **½″, 3″, 8″**; draw lines.

Place dots on the left and right at **2½″, 5½″**; draw lines.

Place dots on the first vertical line at **3½″, 4½″**; draw slanting lines from the left of the paper, through the dots, to the intersection of the second vertical line with the horizontal lines. Place dots on the right at **3½″, 4½″**; draw slanting lines to the inner corners.

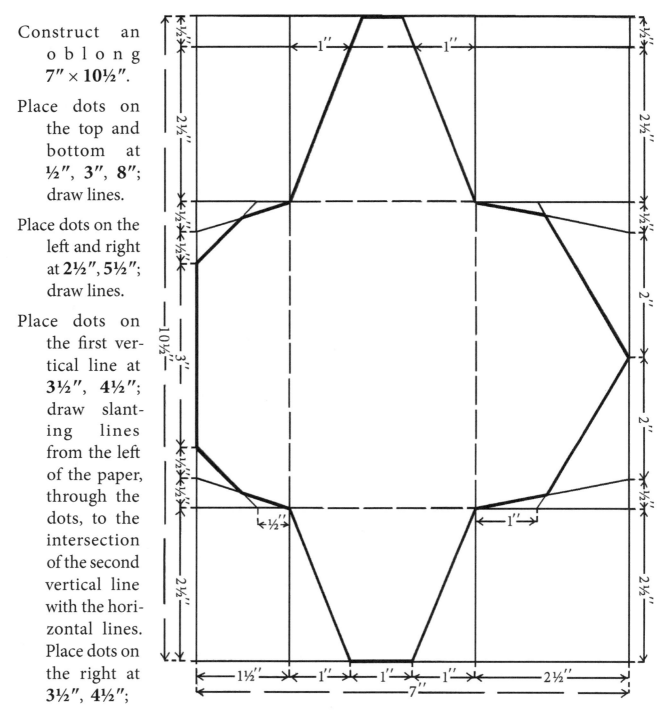

Place dots on the top at **3½″, 5½″, 7½″**; dots on the second and third vertical lines at **1½″, 6″**; draw slanting lines. (See drawing.) Place dots on the bottom at **3½″, 4″, 7″, 7½″**; draw slanting lines. (See drawing.)

Cut, fold, and paste **½″** lap inside.

XI. WALL POCKET. 6″ × 8″ *(Bristol Board)*

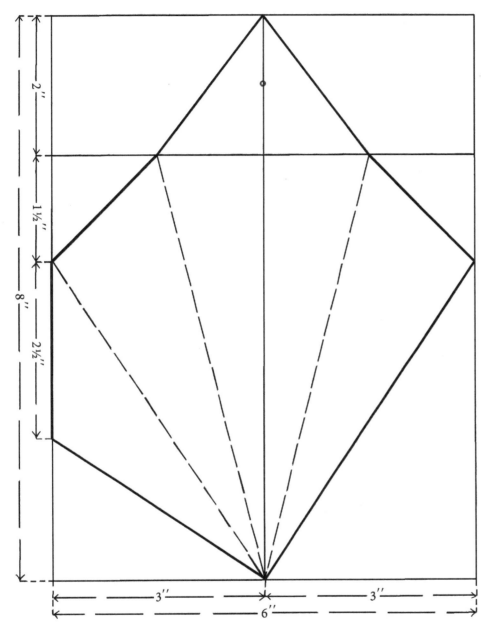

Construct an oblong **6″ × 8″**. Place dots on the top and bottom at **2″**; draw a line. Place dots on the left and right at **3″**; draw a line.

Place dots on the vertical line at **2″**, **4″**; draw to the center point at the left; at the right.

Place a dot on the top at **3½″**; draw a line to the **2″** dot on the vertical line and to the point on the right.

Place dots on the bottom at **3½″**, **6″**; draw to the vertical line and to the point at the right. (See drawing.)

Place a dot on the center line **1″** from left, for the hole. Cut and fold. Paste the lap outside, trimming the edge if necessary.

XII. PICTURE FRAME. 5″ × 10″ *(Royal Melton)*

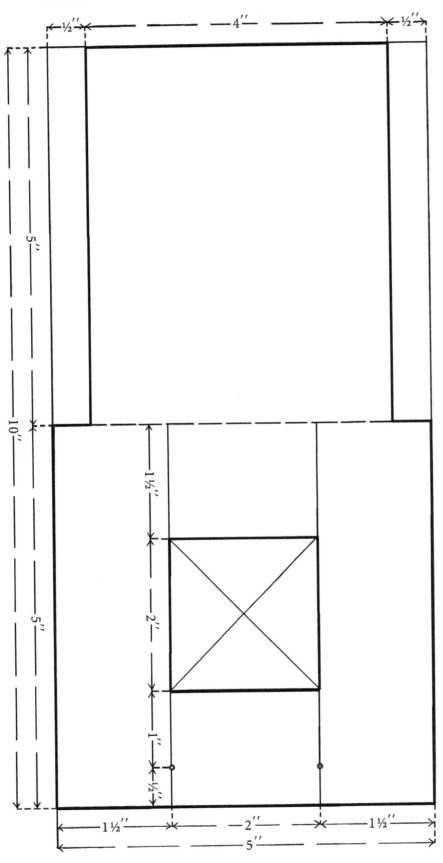

Construct an oblong **5″ × 10″**.

Place dots on the top and bottom at **5″**; draw line.

Place dots on the left and on the vertical line at **½″, 4½″**; draw lines.

Place dots on the vertical line and the right at **1½″, 3½″**; draw lines.

Place dots on the horizontal lines at **1½″, 3½″**; connect the dots.

Draw diagonals in the square.

Punch a hole in the center with the scissors' point; cut on the lines to corners; score outline of the square with scissors, then cut on the lines.

Place dots **½″** from the right on the horizontal lines; fold the paper and punch holes on the dots.

Paste the sides, leaving the top open for a picture.

XIII. RIBBON BOX. 9″ × 11½″

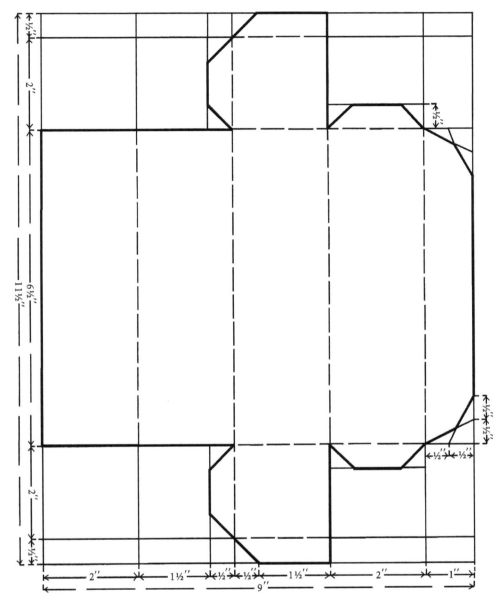

Construct an oblong **9″ × 11½″**. Place dots on the top and bottom at **½″, 2½″, 9″, 11″**; draw lines.

Place dots on the left and right at **1″, 3″, 5″, 7″**; draw lines. Place dots on the top at **3″, 3½″, 8″, 8½″**.

Place dots on the second and third vertical lines at **½″**; draw slanting lines. (See drawing.)

Place dots on the first and second horizontal lines at **2″, 9½″**; draw lines.

Place dots on these lines at **½″, 1½″**; draw to the corners.

Place dots on the left and right at **5½″**. Hold the ruler on the dots, draw a line across the second and fourth spaces.

Place dots on this line at **1″, 2″, 9½″, 10½″**; draw lines to the corners.

Place dots on the left and right at **4½″**; draw lines to the corners.

Cut, fold, and paste the laps inside. Fold the cover laps outside.

XIV. PEN BOX. 4″ × 6″ *(Bristol Board)*

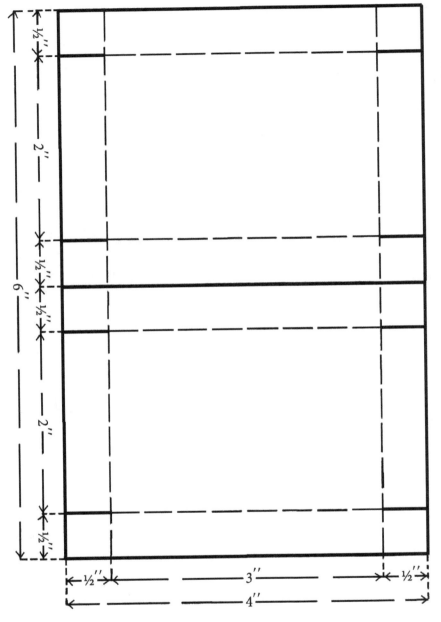

Construct an oblong **4″ × 6″**.

Place dots on the top and bottom at **½″, 2½″, 3″, 3½″, 5½″**; draw lines.

Place dots on the left and right at **½″, 3½″**; draw lines.

Cut on the **3″** line.

Cut, fold, and paste laps inside.

Collar. Construct an oblong **1″ × 10½″**. Cut inside the line so that the collar will be less than **1″** wide.

Fit into the box carefully, creasing the corners, and paste onto the lower half of the box.

The top should fit easily over the collar.

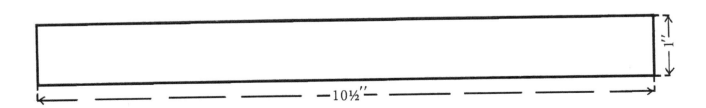

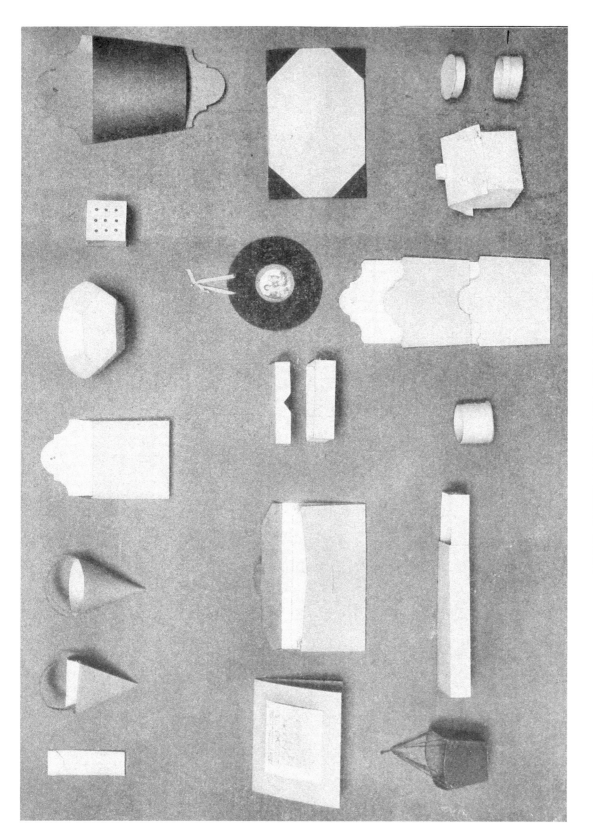

PAPER SLOYD MODELS FOR THE THIRD YEAR

I. POCKET-COMB CASE. 3″ × 5½″

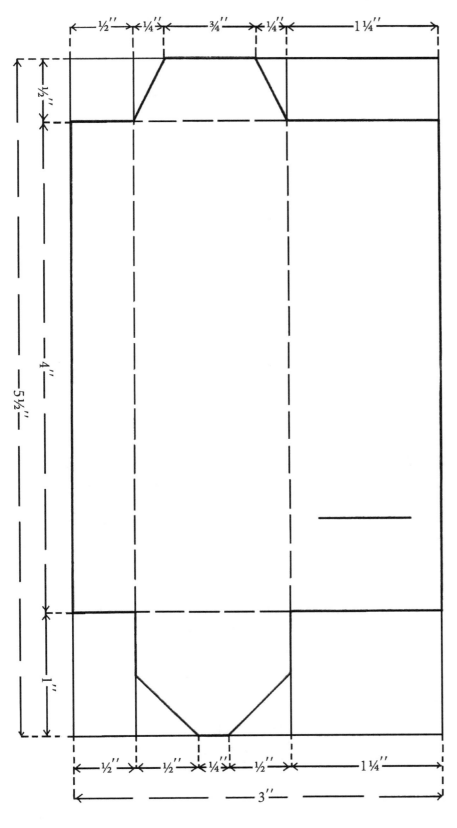

Construct an oblong **3″ × 5½″**.

Place dots on the top and bottom at **½″, 4½″**; draw lines.

Place dots on the left and right at **1¼″, 2½″**; draw lines.

Place dots on left at **1½″, 2¼″**; draw lines to corners.

Place dots on the right at **1¾″, 2″**, and on the horizontal lines at **5″**; draw slanting lines.

Place dots on the top and on the first horizontal line at **3¾″**.

Hold the ruler on the dots and draw from **¼″** to **1″**.

Cut the line with a knife.

Cut, fold, and paste the laps inside, leaving space for the comb.

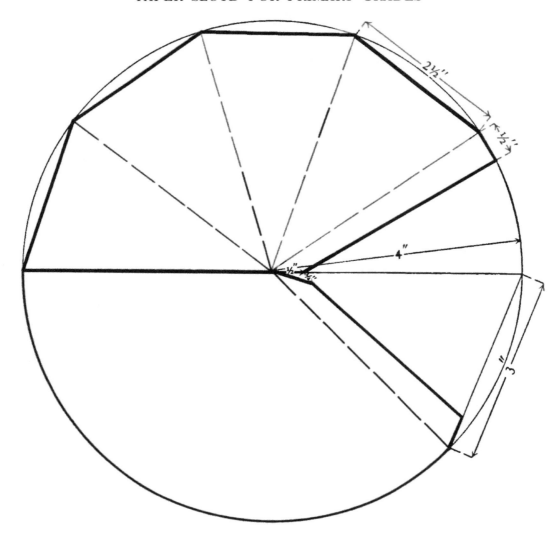

II. PYRAMIDAL CATCH-ALL.
8″ × 8″ *(Bristol Board)*

Draw a horizontal line **8″** long. Place a dot in the middle. Set the compass to **4″** and draw a circle. Set the compass to **2½″**. Begin at the left on the diameter and make four dots on the circumference; draw lines from dot to dot and from each dot to the center. Place dots on the circumference and on the diameter, **½″** to the right of the last line; draw a line. Cut, fold, and paste.

Handle. **1″ × 6″**. Fold and paste. Paste the handle on the inside, in the middle of opposite sides.

III. CONICAL FLOWER HOLDER.
8″ × 8″ *(Bristol Board)*

Place the remaining piece with the diameter horizontal. Set the compass to **3″** and place a dot on the circumference **3″** from the right; draw a line to the center dot. Place a dot on the diameter and on the circumference, **½″** to the right of the line; draw a line. Place a dot on the line **¼″** from the diameter; draw a line to the center. Cut, fold, and paste.

Handle. **1″ × 6″**. Fold and paste. Paste the handle inside on the lap and on the opposite side.

IV. POSTAL-CARD HOLDER. 6″ × 11¼″

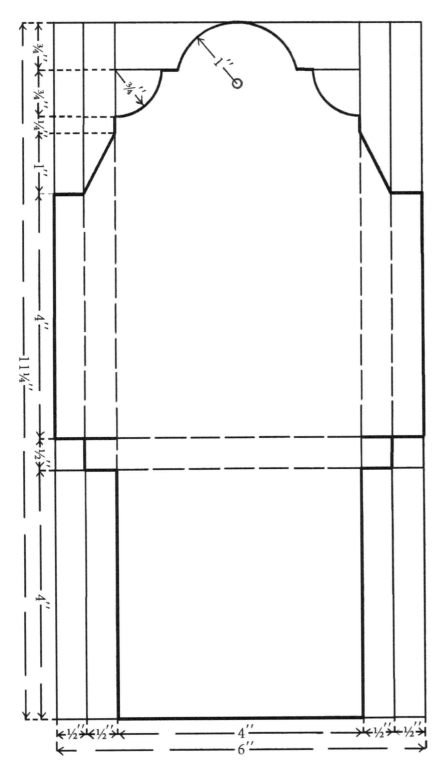

Construct an oblong **6″ × 11¼″**.

Place dots on the top and bottom at **6¾″, 7¼″**; draw lines.

Place dots on the left and right at **½″, 1″, 5″, 5½″**; draw lines.

Place dots on the second and third horizontal lines at **¾″, 1″, 1½″, 1¾″**.

Connect **¾″** dots with light line.

Set compass to **¾″**.

Place the point on the first dots; draw curves from vertical line to **1½″** dots.

Hold the ruler on the **1″** dots; make a dot at **3″**.

Set the compass to **1″**; draw a curve.

Place dots on the first and fourth horizontal lines at **2¾″**; draw straight lines across the outside spaces, and slanting lines to **1¾″** dots.

Punch a hole.

Cut, fold, and paste laps inside.

V. HEXAGONAL TRAY. 6″ × 6″
(Bristol Board)

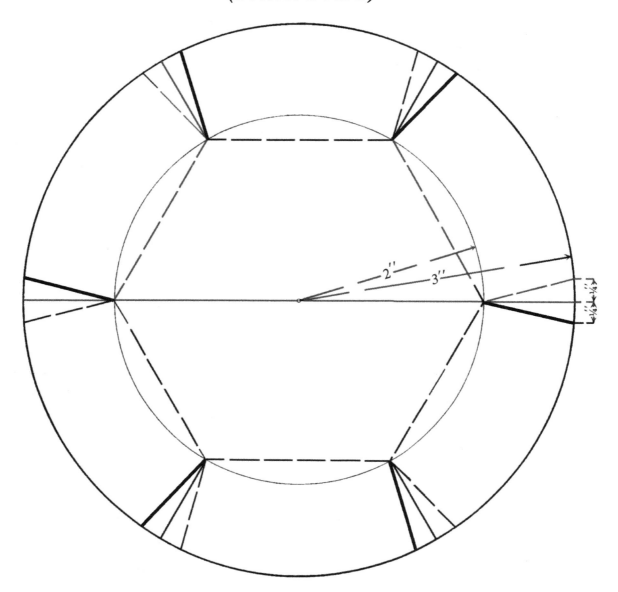

Draw a horizontal line **6″** long and place a dot in the middle.

Set the compass to **3″**; draw a circle. Set the compass to **2″**; draw a circle.

Begin on the horizontal line and with the compass divide the inner circle into six equal parts. Place the ruler on the opposite dots and draw slanting lines to the outer circle.

Place dots on the circumference ¼″ on each side of the lines; draw lines to the dots on the inner circle.

Draw a hexagon inside the inner circle.

Cut, fold, and paste the laps outside.

VI. PIN CUBE. 7" × 8½"

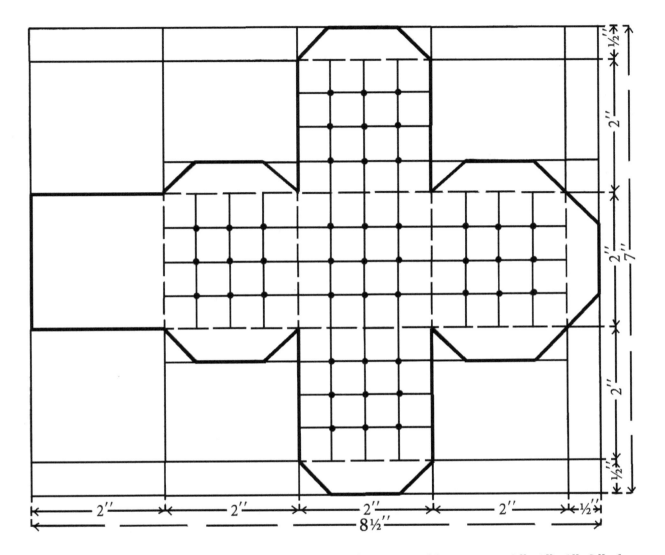

Construct an oblong **7" × 8½"**. Place dots on the top and bottom at **2", 4", 6", 8"**; draw lines. Place dots on the left and right at **½", 2½", 4½", 6½"**; draw lines.

Place dots on the first and fourth horizontal lines at **4½", 5", 5½"**; draw lines. Place dots on the second and third horizontal lines at **2½", 3", 3½", 6½", 7", 7½"**; draw lines.

Place dots on the first and fourth vertical lines at **2", 3", 3½", 4", 5"**; draw lines.

Place dots on the second and third vertical lines at **1", 1½", 5½", 6"**; draw lines.

Place a ruler across the corners of the squares and draw the slanting lines across the narrow spaces. (See drawing.)

Make dots at the intersection of lines in the squares. Prick dots with a pin.

Cut, fold, and paste the laps inside. Stick pins in the holes.

VII. WHISK-BROOM HOLDER

BACK. 6½″ × 10″ *(Bristol Board)*

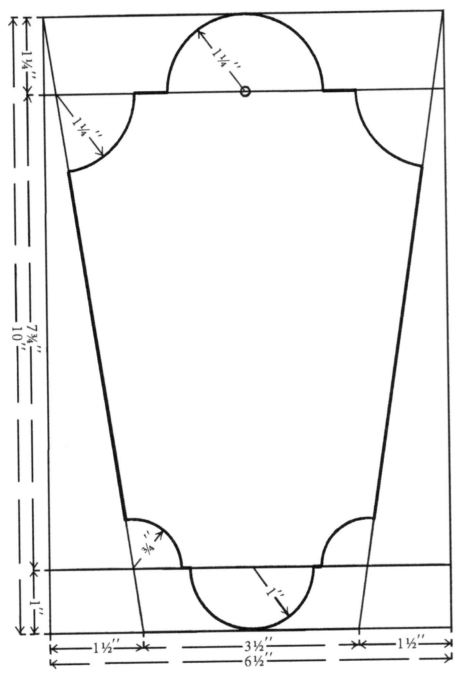

Construct an oblong **6½″ × 10″**. Place dots on the top and bottom at **1¼″, 9″**; draw lines.

Place dots on the right at **1½″, 5″**; draw slanting lines from the left upper and lower corners to the dots.

Place a dot on the first vertical line at **3¼″**. Set the compass to **1¼″**; draw a half circle.

Place the point of the compass at the intersection of the vertical lines with the slanting lines; draw curves.

Place a dot on the second vertical line at **3¼″**. Set the compass to **1″**; draw a half circle. Set the compass to **¾″**; draw curves. (See drawing.)

Punch the hole. Cut the straight lines first, then the curves.

VII. WHISK-BROOM HOLDER

POCKET. 4¾″ × 8″ *(Bristol Board)*

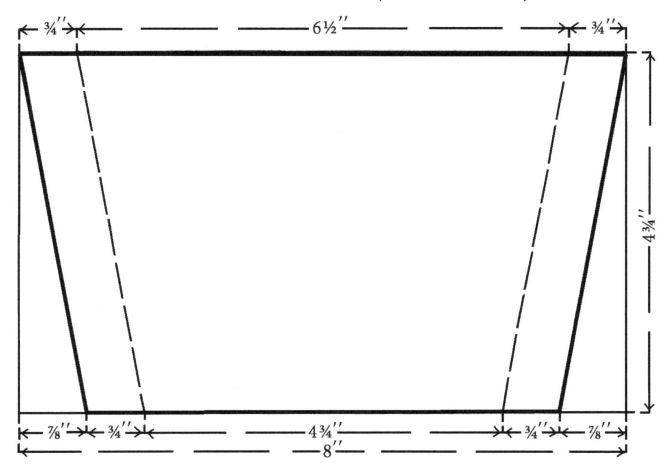

Construct an oblong of bristol board **4¾″ × 8″**.

Place dots on the top at **¾″**, **7¼″**; on the bottom at **⅞″**, **1⅝″**, **6⅜″**, **7⅛″**; draw slanting lines.

Cut, fold, and paste onto the back **½″** below the curve, with laps outside.

VIII. MEASURE. 1″ × 6″
(Bristol Board)

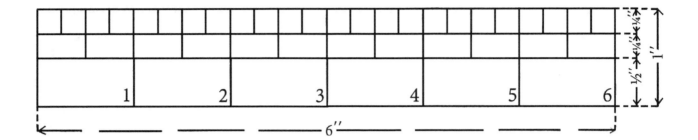

Construct an oblong **1″ × 6″**.

Place dots on the top and bottom at every inch mark; draw lines.

Place dots on the left and right at ¼″, ½″; draw lines.

Place dots at every ½″ mark on the top and second horizontal line; draw lines.

Place dots at every ¼″ mark on the top and first horizontal line; draw lines.

IX. CALENDAR LEAVES. 3⅛″ × 3⅝″
(Foolscap Paper)

Construct an oblong of foolscap paper **9** lines wide, **3⅝″** long.

Place dots on the first and seventh lines at ½″, ⅞″, 1¼″, 1⅝″, 2″, 2⅜″, 2¾″, 3⅛″; draw lines.

Trace the first, second, and seventh lines with a pencil; draw a line through the middle of the first and the second spaces.

Print the name of the month and year in the first space, the first letters of the days of the week in the second space, and fill the other spaces with the correct figures.

Paste or sew the leaves together at the top.

IX. CALENDAR BACK. 5⅝″ × 12″
(Bristol Board)

Construct an oblong **5⅝″ × 12″**.

Place dots on the top and bottom at **4½″, 9¼″, 11½″**; draw lines.

Fold and paste the lap inside.

Paste the leaves of the calendar together at the top, finishing with the first month.

Paste the calendar onto the back with a space of **1″** on each side and ¾″ at the top.

	20	JANUARY			20	
S	M	T	W	T	F	S

3⅛″

½″ ⅜″

3⅝″

X. EXTENSION ENVELOPE FOR
CLIPPINGS. 9¼″ × 11½″

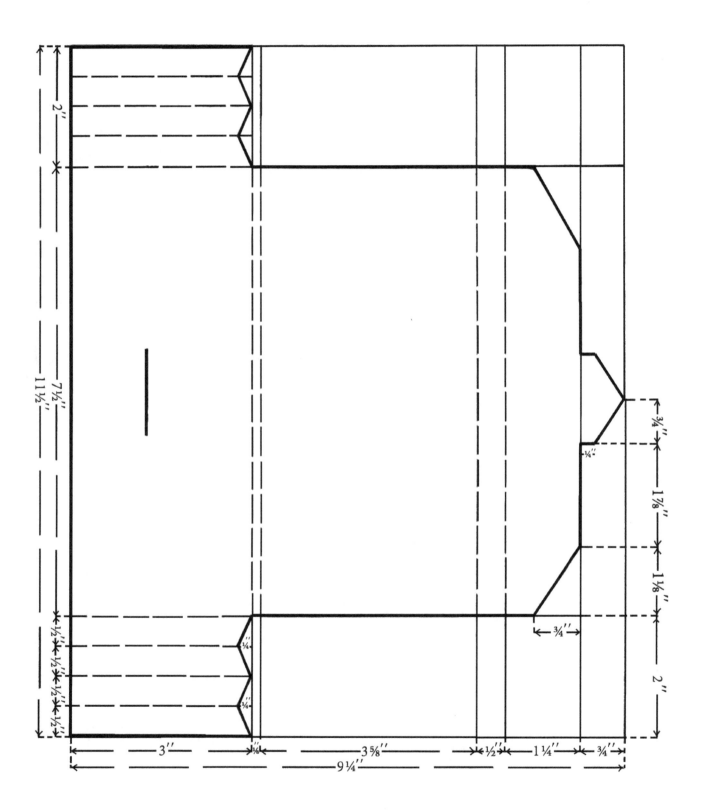

X. EXTENSION ENVELOPE FOR CLIPPINGS. 9¼″ × 11½″

Construct an oblong **9¼″ × 11½″**.

Place dots on the top and bottom at **2″, 9½″**; draw lines.

Place dots on the left and right at **¾″, 2″, 2½″, 6⅛″, 6¼″**; draw lines.

Place dots on the last horizontal line and at the bottom at **½″, 1″, 1½″, 10″, 10½″, 11″**; draw lines.

Place dots on the first and third lines, on both sides, at **¼″**; draw to the dots. (See drawing.)

Place dots on the vertical lines at **8½″**; hold a ruler on the dots and draw a line from **3″** to **4½″**.

Cut the line with a knife.

Place dots on the top at **5″, 5¾″, 6½″**.

Place dots on the first horizontal line at **3⅛″, 5″, 6½″, 8⅜″**; on the vertical lines at **1½″**.

Draw lines across the corners.

Draw from the **5″** and **6½″** dots on the horizontal line to the dots on the top.

Place dots on the lines at **½″**; draw lines to the point.

Cut, fold, and paste the laps inside.

XI. BOX WITH COVER *(Bristol Board)*

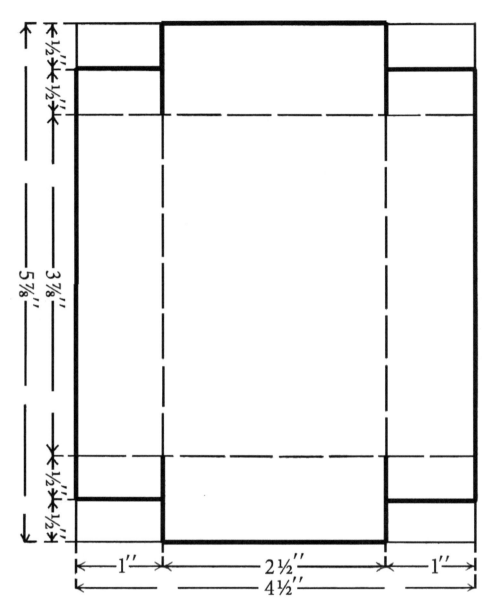

Box. 4½″ × 5⅞″

Construct an oblong
  4½″ × 5⅞″.

Place dots on the top
  and bottom at **1″**,
  4⅞″; draw lines.

Place dots on the left
  and right at **1″**,
  3½″; draw lines.

Place dots on the top
  and bottom at **½″**,
  5⅜″; draw lines
  across the narrow
  spaces.

Cut, fold, and paste the
  laps inside.

XI. BOX WITH COVER *(Bristol Board)*

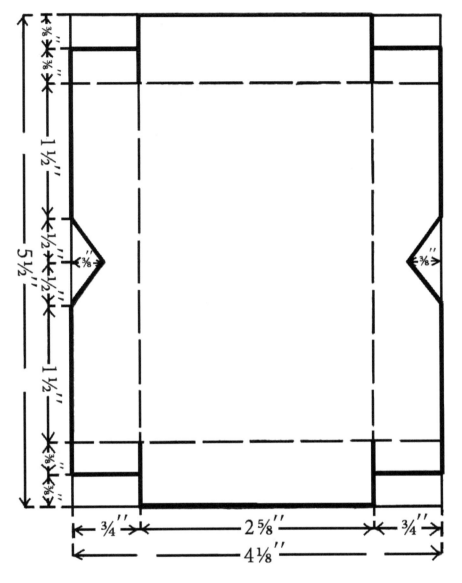

Cover. 4⅛″ × 5½″

Construct an oblong **4⅛″ × 5½″**.

Place dots on the top and bottom at **¾″, 4¾″**; draw lines.

Place dots on the left and right at **¾″, 3⅜″**; draw lines.

Place dots on the top and bottom at **⅜″, 2¼″, 2¾″, 3¼″, 5⅛″**. Hold the ruler on the first dots and the last dots and draw lines across the narrow spaces.

Hold the ruler on the middle dots and make dots at **⅜″, 3¾″**; draw slanting lines. (See drawing.)

Cut, fold, and paste laps inside. Cut slanting lines.

XII. ROUND FRAME. 5″ × 5″ (*Royal Melton*)

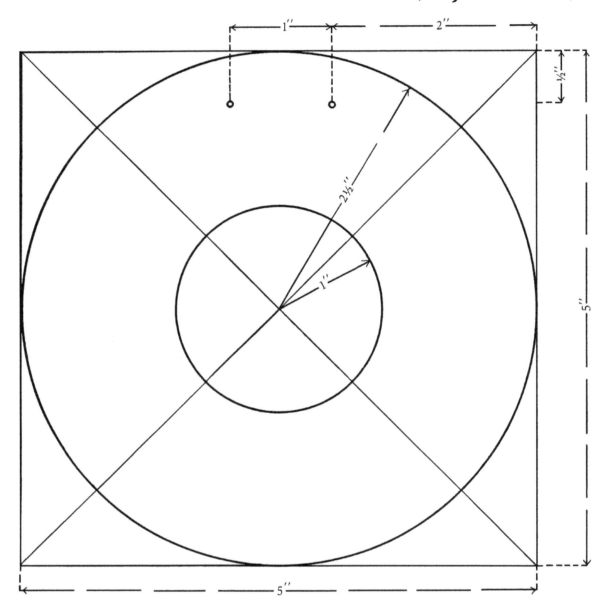

Construct a square **5″ × 5″**. Draw diagonals. Set the compass to **1″**, to **2½″**, and draw the circles.

Place dots on the left and right at **½″**; hold the ruler on the dots and place dots at **2″**, **3″**; punch holes for tie.

Make a hole with the scissors at the center of the circle. Cut on the diagonals of the inner circle, then cut on the circle. Cut the outer circle.

Back. 3″ × 3″. Construct a square **3″ × 3″**. Fit this square onto the back, the corners touching the diagonals.

Paste at the bottom and the sides.

XIII. BLOTTING PAD

BACK. 5⅛″ × 7⅞″ (*Bristol Board*)

COVER FOR BACK. 5″ × 7¾″ (*Manila Drawing*)

BLOTTER. 5″ × 7¾″

CORNER. 1¼″ × 2½″ (*Royal Melton or other cover paper*)

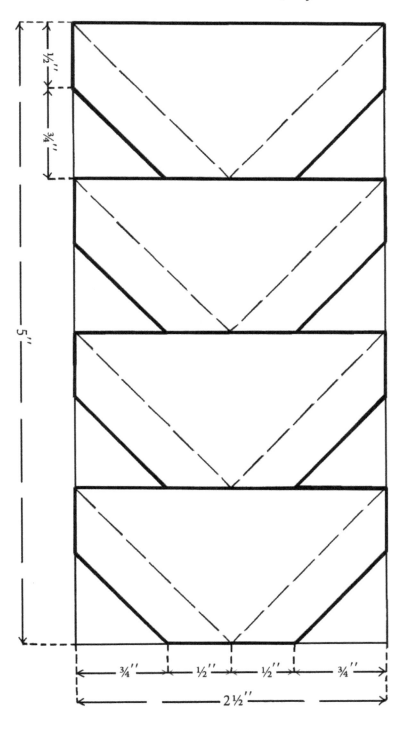

Corners. Construct an oblong **2½″ × 5″**.

Place dots on the top and bottom at **1¼″, 2½″, 3¾″**; draw lines.

Place dots on the first line and at the right at **¾″, 1¼″, 1¾″**. Hold the ruler on the dots, and place dots on each vertical line.

Place dots on the top and bottom at **½″, 1¾″, 3″, 4¼″**; draw slanting lines. (See drawing.)

Cut. Place the blotter on top of the back.

Fold the laps of the corners and paste the same to the back.

Paste the cover paper over the back.

Corner pieces may be of thin paper covered with cloth. Heavy paper or tin corners of the same size to be used on corners of books sent in the mails, may be constructed by using paper or tin **1¼″** in width.

XIV. TWINE HOLDER. 6¾" × 6¾" *(Bristol Board)*

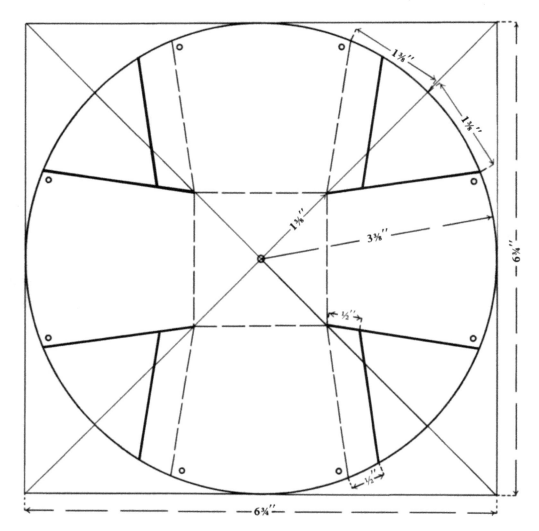

Construct a square **6¾" × 6¾"**. Draw the diagonals of the square.

Set the compass to **3⅜"**; draw a circle. Set the compass to **1⅜"** and place dots on the diagonals; connect the dots.

Set the compass to **1⅜"** and place the point at the intersection of the diagonals with the circle; place dots on the circumference on each side of the diagonals; draw lines from these dots to the corners of the inner square.

Set the compass to **½"**. Place dots on the circle and on the slanting lines; connect the dots. (See drawing.)

Punch a hole in the center for the end of the ball of twine. Place dots in the corners for holes. Cut, fold, and paste the laps inside. Punch holes.

Tie with cords at each corner or with cords from opposite sides.

The basket may be used for matches if the hole is not punched in the center.

XV. SLIDING PENCIL BOX. *(Bristol Board)*

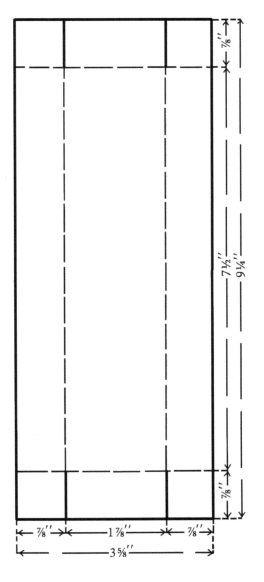

Box

Construct an oblong **3⅝″ × 9¼″**.

Place dots on the top and bottom at **⅞″, 8⅜″**; draw lines.

Place dots on the left and right at **⅞″, 2¾″**; draw lines.

Cut, fold, and paste the laps inside.

Case

Construct an oblong **6⅞″ × 7½″**.

Place dots on the left and right at **⅞″, 2⅞″, 3⅞″, 5⅞″**; draw lines.

Fold and paste the ⅞″ lap inside.

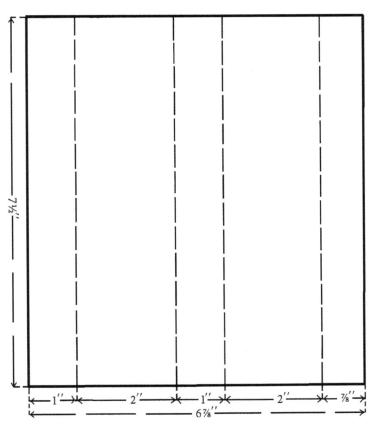

XVI. MATCH HOLDER. 2⅛″ × 6⅜″ *(Bristol Board)*

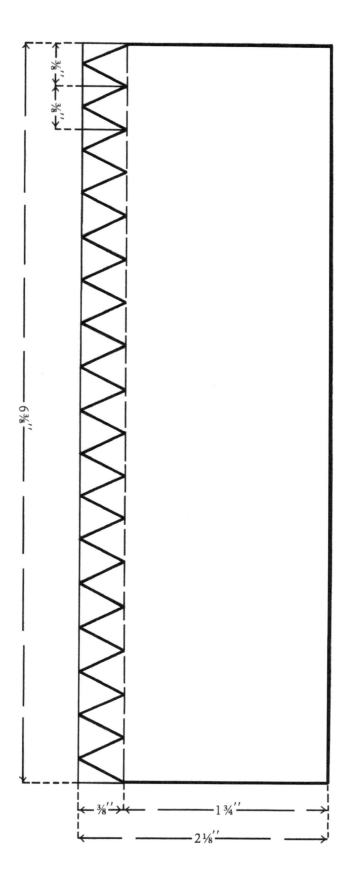

Side

Construct an oblong **2⅛″ × 6⅜″**.

Place dots on the left and right at **1¾″**; draw a line.

Beginning at the left, place dots on the line every ⅜″, and on the bottom at ³⁄₁₆″, then every ⅜″; draw points.

Fold on the line, then cut the points.

XVI. MATCH HOLDER. 2⅛″ × 6⅜″ *(Bristol Board)*

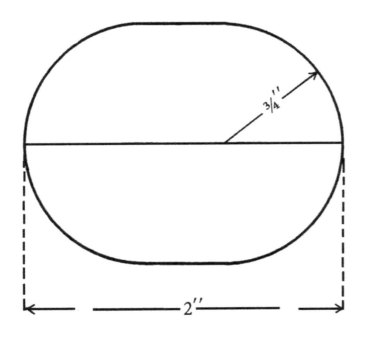

Bottom (inside)

1½″ × 2″

Draw a horizontal line **2″** long.

Place dots at **¾″, 1¼″**.

Set the compass to **¾″**; draw two half circles; connect the curved lines.

Cut.

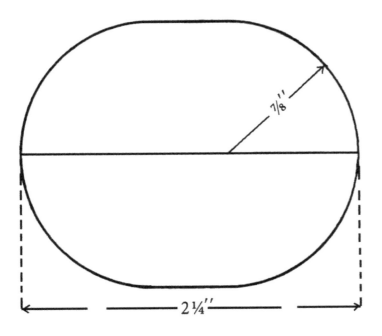

Bottom (outside)

1¾″ × 2¼″

Draw a horizontal line **2¼″** long.

Place dots at **⅞″, 1⅜″**.

Set the compass to **⅞″**; draw two half circles; connect the curved lines.

Cut.

Paste the edge of the inside piece over the points.

Paste the bottom over all.

Paste the lap on the side.

A piece **¼″ × 6⅜″** pasted around the top, even at the edge, will strengthen the holder.

XVII. LETTER HOLDER. *(Bristol Board)*

BACK. 4½″ × 10¾″

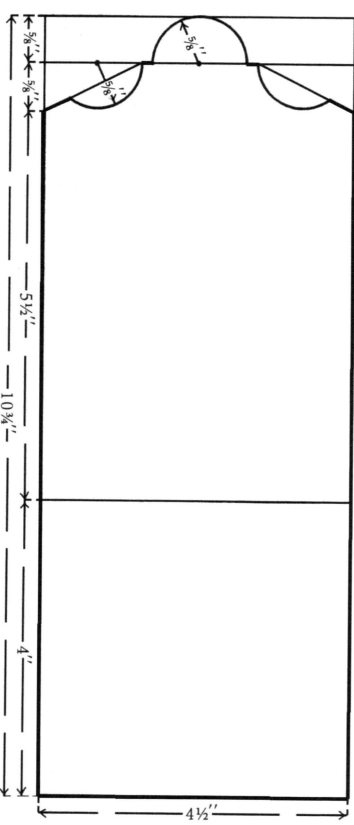

Construct an oblong **4½″ × 10¾″**.

Place dots on the top and bottom at **⅝″, 6¾″**; draw lines.

Place dots on the first line at **⅝″, 2¼″, 3⅞″**.

Set the compass to **⅝″**; place it on the center dot and draw a half circle; on the other dots and draw the curves.

Place dots on the top and bottom at **1¼″**.

Draw from the dots to the vertical line, touching the ends of the curves.

Cut.

Paste one pocket on the bottom with all the laps folded over the edge onto the back, and the other pocket on the line with the side laps folded over the edge onto the back.

XVII. LETTER HOLDER. *(Bristol Board)*

POCKET. 4⅞″ × 6¼″

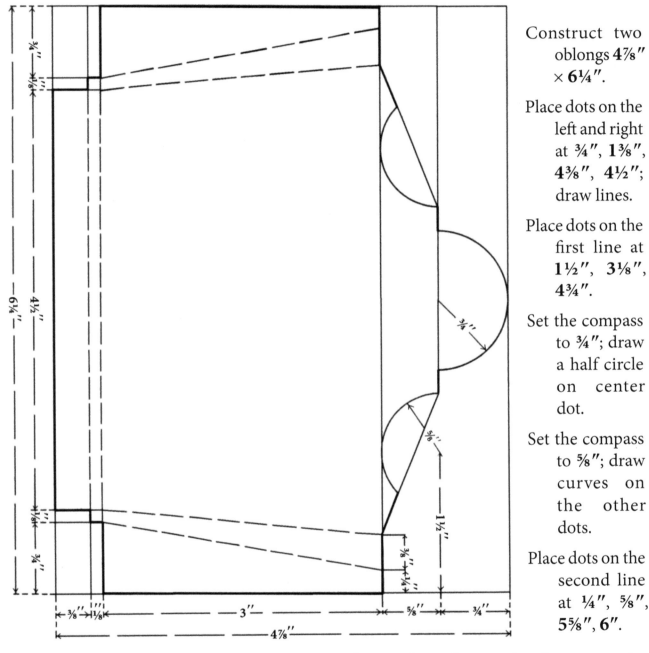

Construct two oblongs 4⅞″ × 6¼″.

Place dots on the left and right at ¾″, 1⅜″, 4⅜″, 4½″; draw lines.

Place dots on the first line at 1½″, 3⅛″, 4¾″.

Set the compass to ¾″; draw a half circle on center dot.

Set the compass to ⅝″; draw curves on the other dots.

Place dots on the second line at ¼″, ⅝″, 5⅝″, 6″.

Draw slanting lines from ends of curves to the second and third dots.

Place dots on the third line and on the bottom at ¾″, ⅞″, 5⅜″, 5½″; connect these dots. Draw slanting lines at the sides. (See drawing.)

XVIII. BANK. 6½″ × 11¼″

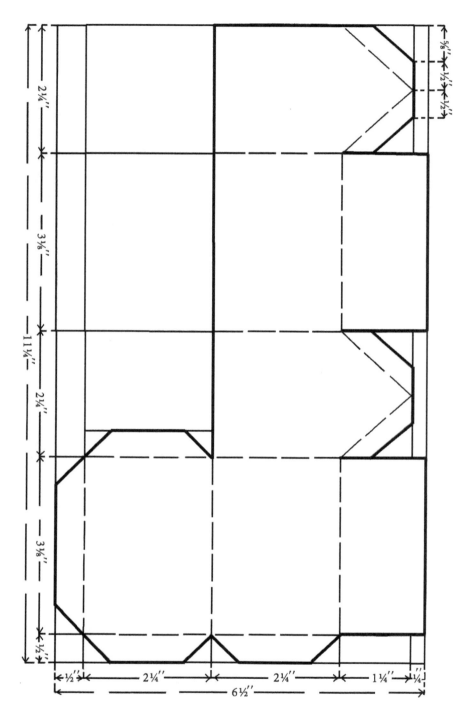

Construct an oblong **6½″ × 11¼″**. Place dots on the top and bottom at **2¼″, 5⅜″, 7⅝″, 10¾″**; draw lines. Place dots on the left and right at **¼″, 1½″, 3¾″, 6″**.

Draw the first line across the first and third spaces, the second line across the second and fourth spaces, and the other lines from dot to dot.

Place dots on the first line at **⅝″, 1⅛″, 1⅝″, 6″, 6½″, 7″**.

Place dots on the left and on the first, second, and third vertical lines at **1″**.

Draw slanting lines from dot to dot. (See drawing.)

Place dots on the third and fourth horizontal lines at **7⅛″**; draw a line. Place dots on this line at **½″, 1¾″**; draw slanting lines to corners.

Place dots on right edge at **2″, 3¼″, 4¼″, 5½″**. Draw lines to corners. (See drawing.) Cut, fold, and paste the laps inside.

XVIII. BANK

CHIMNEY. ½″ × 2½″

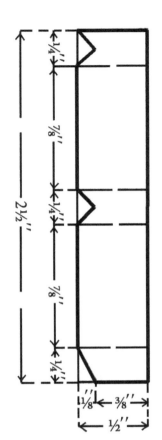

Construct an oblong ½″ × 2½″. Place dots on the top and bottom at ¼″, 1⅛″, 1⅜″, 2¼″; draw lines. Place a dot on the left and right at ⅜″.

Hold the ruler on the dots and place dots on the vertical lines at ⅛″, 1¼″; draw slanting lines. (See drawing.)

Cut, fold, and paste the lap inside. Paste onto the bank roof.

ROOF. 3⅞″ × 4½″

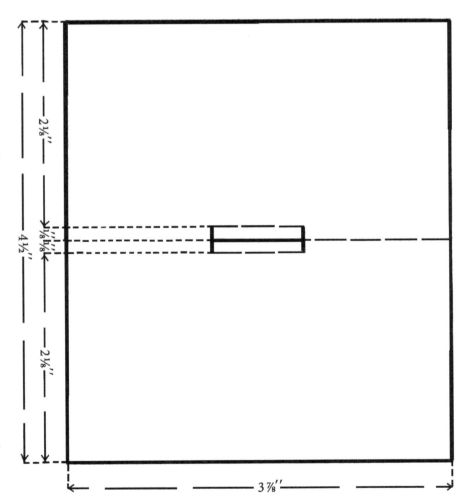

Construct an oblong 3⅞″ × 4½″. Place dots on the top and bottom at 2⅛″, 2¼″, 2⅜″.

Draw a line through the second dots.

Hold a ruler on the first dots and the third dots, and draw from 1½″ to 2⅜″.

Draw horizontal lines across the space. Fold on the middle line.

Cut the horizontal lines, then the center line. Fold the laps back. Paste the roof onto the bank, and the chimney onto the roof—laps inside of the chimney.

I. QUARTERFOIL. 3⅞″ × 3⅞″ *(Bristol Board)*

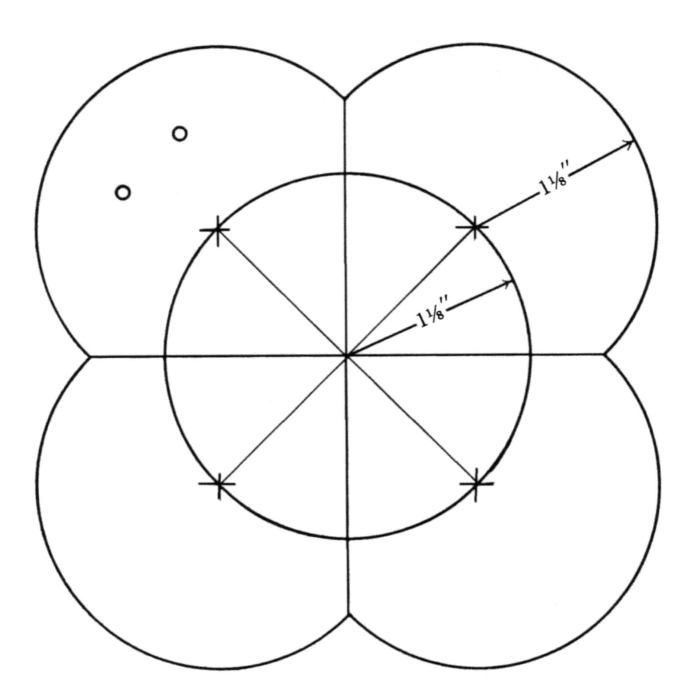

A circle or a square of sandpaper **2¼″** in diameter may be pasted onto the quarterfoil and the same used as a match strike or pencil sharpener.

The inner circle may be cut out and the quarterfoil then used for a picture frame.

A picture or calendar may be pasted over the center.

II. ROUND BUTTON BOX. 1½″ × 6¾″

(Bristol Board)

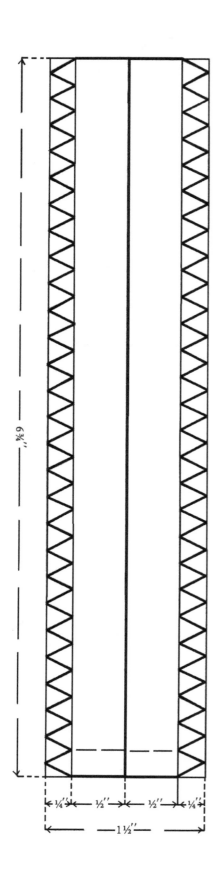

Box. Construct an oblong **1½″ × 6¾″**. Place dots on the left and right at ¼″, ¾″, 1¼″; draw lines. Place dots on the first and third lines, beginning at the left, at every ¼″ mark. Place dots on the top and bottom, beginning at the left at ⅛″, then at every ¼″ mark; draw points. Fold on the first and third lines. Cut the points. Cut the center line.

Bottom and Top (inside). Draw and cut two circles **2″** in diameter.

Bottom and Top (outside). Draw and cut two circles **2¼″** in diameter. Paste the sides of the box, paste the points onto the small circle, then cover with the larger circle. The top and bottom are to be the same.

Collar. Construct an oblong **⅞″ × 6¾″**. The top and bottom of the box being finished, fit and paste the collar onto the lower half of the box.

III. TRIANGULAR CANDY BOX. 8¼″ × 9″

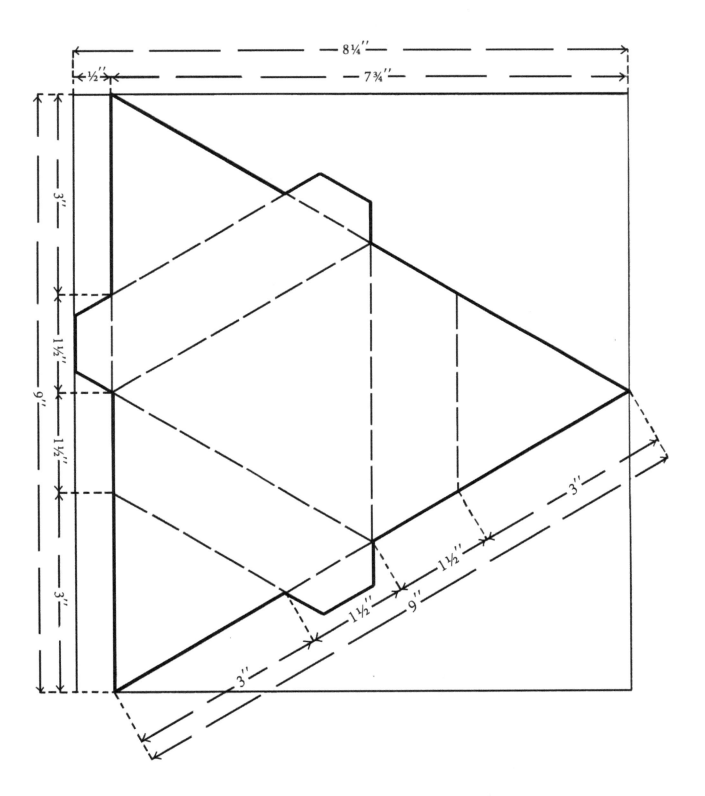

IV. SILK WINDER. 2″ × 2″ × 2″

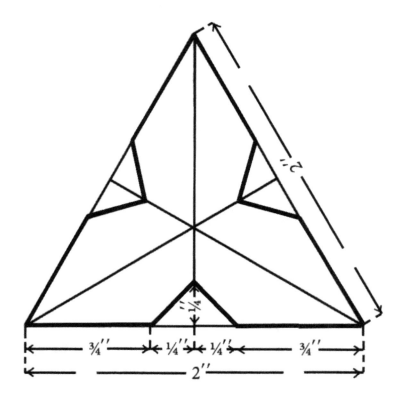

V. SILK WINDER. 2″

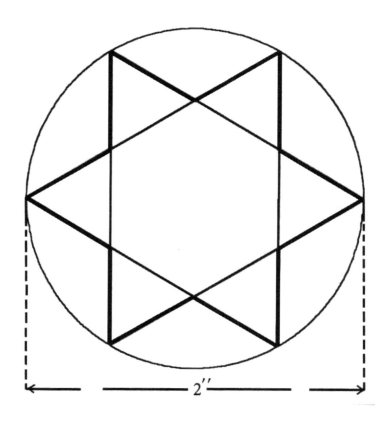

VI. DOLL-HOUSE CHAIR. 6″ × 6″

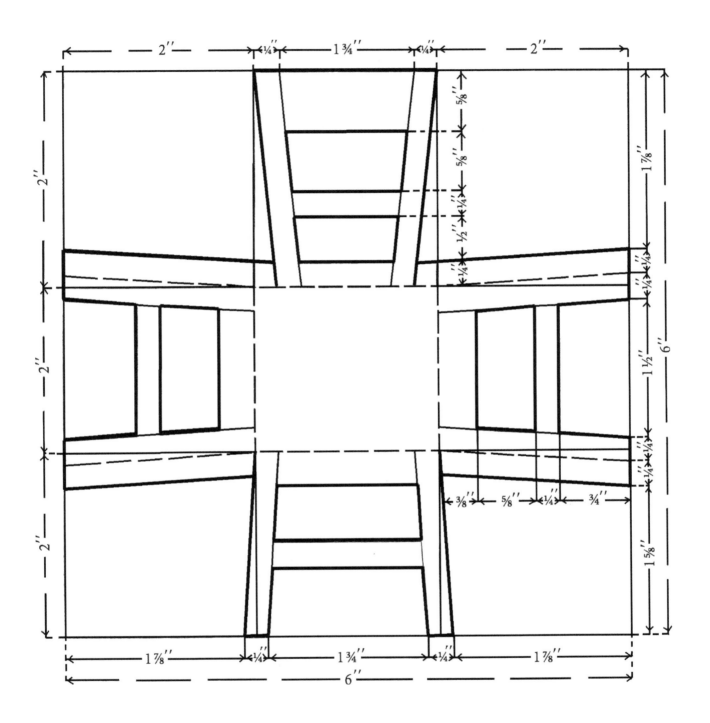

VII. BOOKMARK (ROSETTE). 2″ × 5½″

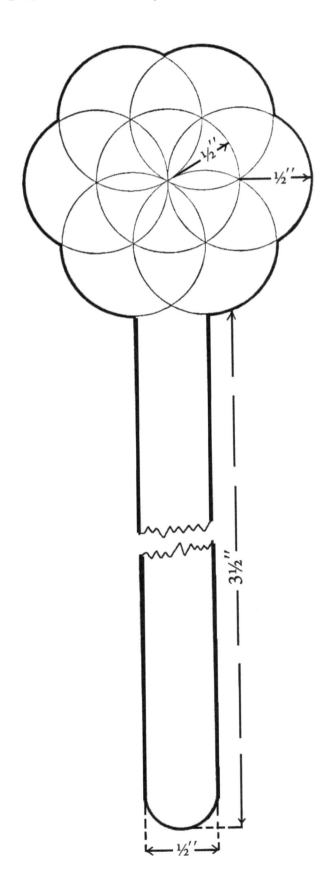

VIII. DOLL-HOUSE TABOURET. 3″ × 5″

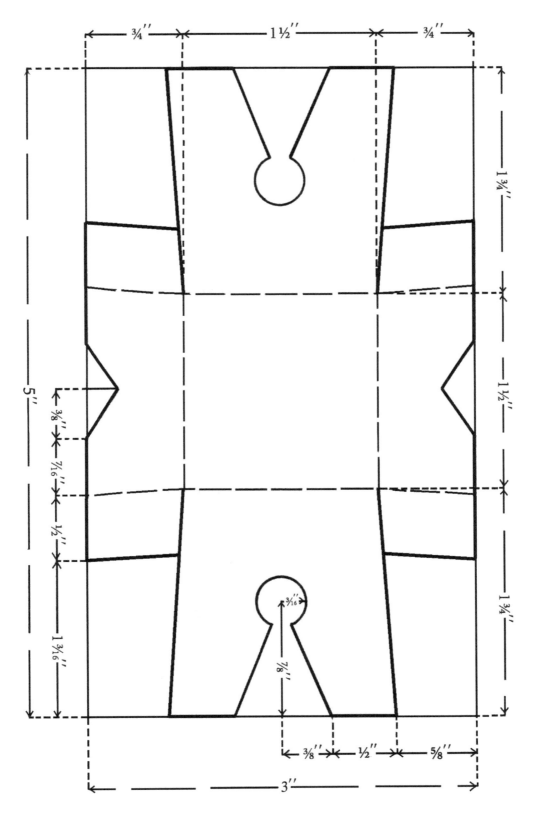

The top of the tabouret may be a circle or an octagon, with the diameter **2″**.

IX. CALENDAR BACK (Pentagon)

Diameter, 4½″

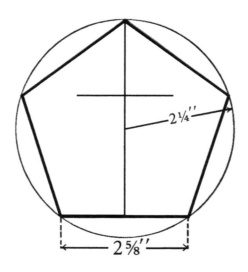

SUPPORT. 2″ × 3″

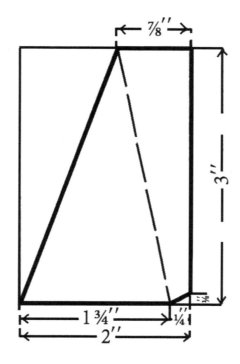

X. PENWIPER

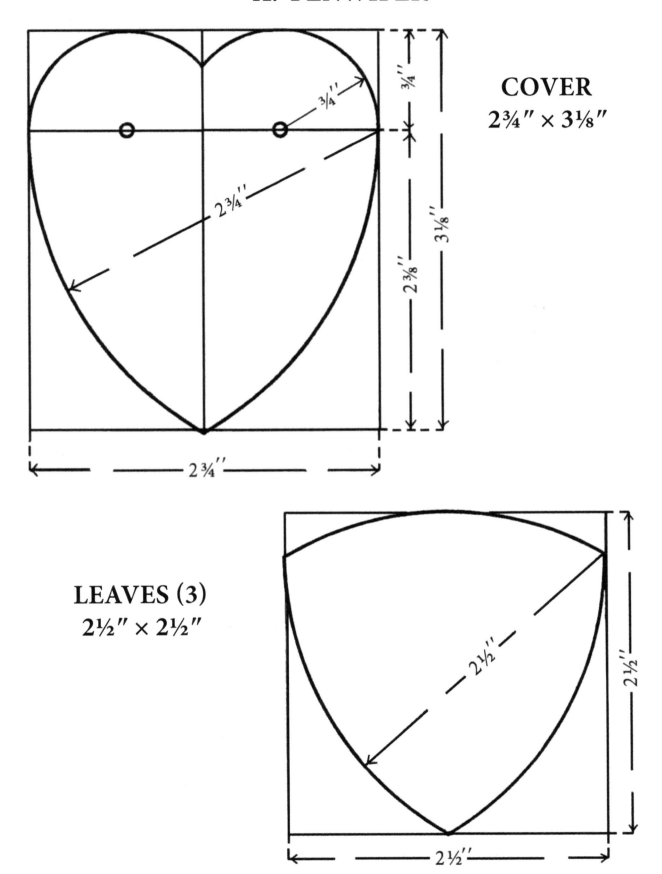

COVER
2¾″ × 3⅛″

¾″

¾″

2¾″

3⅛″

2⅜″

2¾″

LEAVES (3)
2½″ × 2½″

2½″

2½″

2½″

XI. CALENDAR BACK (Trefoil). 4¼″ × 4¼″

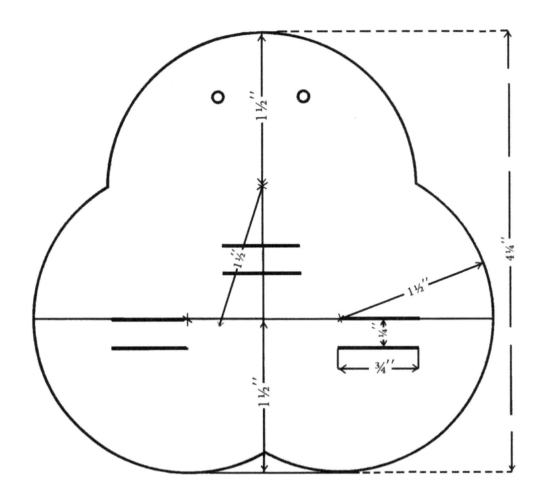

MONTHS OF THE YEAR ⅝″ × 8″

DAYS OF THE WEEK ⅝″ × 8″

DAYS OF THE MONTH ⅝″ × 9½″

XII. DIAMOND-SHAPED BOX

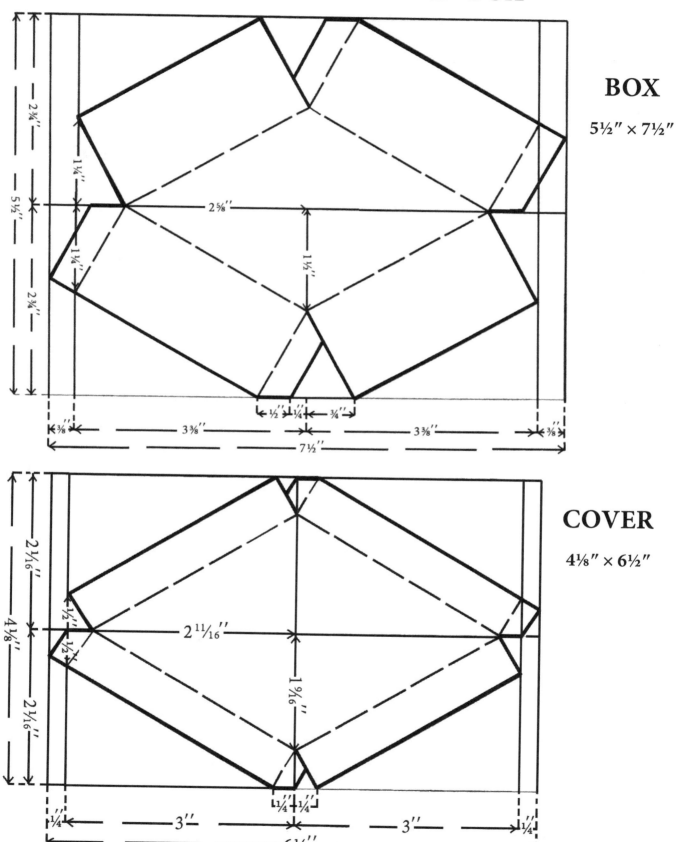

BOX

5½″ × 7½″

COVER

4⅛″ × 6½″

XIII. LETTER BOX. 6″ × 11½″

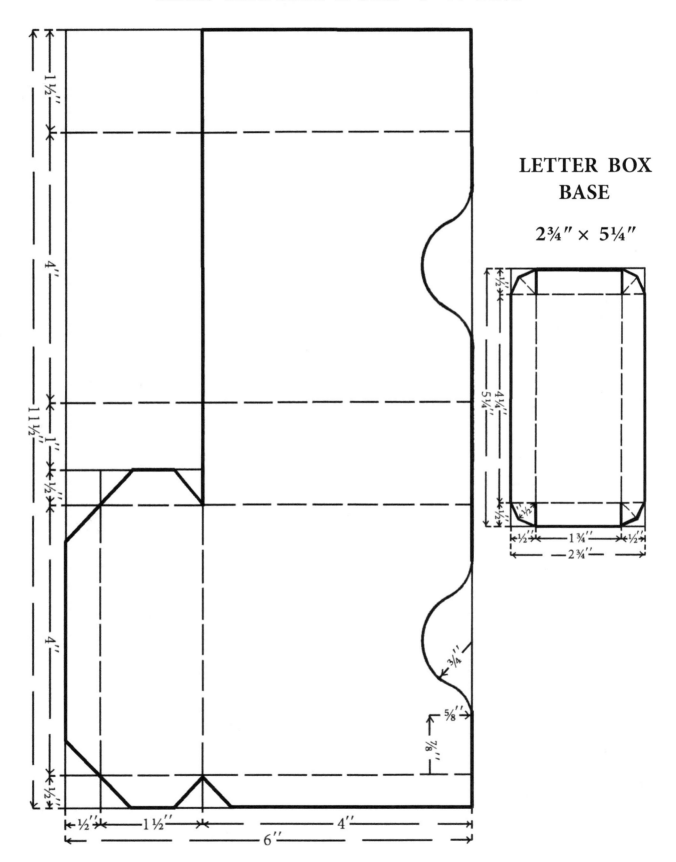

LETTER BOX
BASE

2¾″ × 5¼″

XIV. BOOKMARK. 2″ × 6″

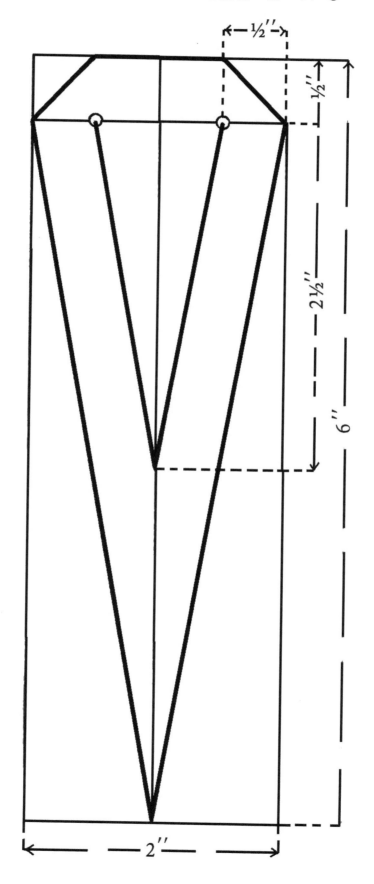

CPSIA information can be obtained
at www.ICGtesting.com
Printed in the USA
BVHW052025240920
589466BV00008B/303